HOW TO MASTER
BASEBALL

By
Winston B. Lewy

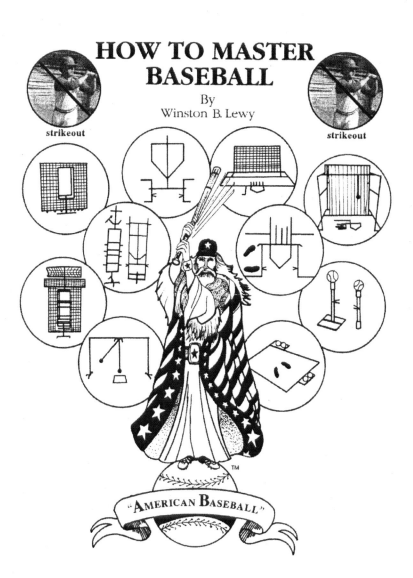

strikeout

strikeout

"AMERICAN BASEBALL"

HOW TO MASTER BASEBALL

BASEBALL + BAT MASTER = HOME RUN

WINSTON B. LEWY

To order additional copies of this book, contact:
Xlibris Corporation
1-888-795-4274
www.Xlibris.com
Orders@Xlibris.com
18036

ACKNOWLEDGMENT

To my generous, loving Father; kind, patient Brother "J"; beautiful, adorable Mother Mary; and helpful Step-Father "J", for all their support in making this book possible. Were it not for them, I would have given up a long time ago. They helped me from the beginning and would not let me quit. Without their ideas, these inventions and book would not have been imaginable. I cannot thank them enough for all their help. To my loving daughter, Francesca, who was very patient, kind and understanding. In Memory of Helen Olson. Also, a thank you to Albert Garcia at N2 Graphics, Pasadena, CA.

DEDICATION

*TO ALL THE BASEBALL PLAYERS AND ANYONE ELSE WHO
LOVES BASEBALL*

To all my soldiers who will take the first step in changing their way of hitting the ball. So when they step up to the plate they will say, "I will never strike out again; and if I do, I will use the Tee Masters, Bat Master, Home Plate, Backstop Master, Bat Speed Apparatus, and Stance and Stride Device and go practice, practice."

To all my soldiers who will take the first step in changing their way of throwing the ball. So when they pick up the ball they will say, "I will not mis-throw the ball; and if I do, I will use the Stepping Square, Bat Speed Apparatus, Super Strike Master 2 (SSM2), and Super Strike Master Junior (SSMJ) and go practice, practice."

To all my soldiers who will take the first step in changing their way of sliding into base and say, "If I am put out while sliding into base, I will use the Slide Master and go practice, practice."

To all my soldiers who want to practice infield or outfield by themselves, use the Super Strike Master 1 (SSM1) or Super Strike Master Junior (SSMJ) and go practice, practice.

CONTENTS

INTRODUCTION

Q. Why did you write this baseball book?

A. I wrote this book because I felt it was time to present a proper method of teaching a player how to hit. For example, when a Major League player got up to bat with a record of five hits for forty-one times at bat, or had been put out thirty-six times, that really upset me. While looking at the batter swinging helplessly at the ball, and the pitcher having no trouble in striking him/her out, I said, "It's time for a change!" I want the batter to have the knowledge so that he/she will not be scared at the plate. So that he/she will not strikeout and will be able to hit the ball such a distance that they will have to move the home run fence back, instead of forward like they are doing today. Boys, girls, men and women, this book is for you. I hope you will take the first step and believe me when I say, "It's time for a change to have one proper method in the way a player hits, throws, and plays the various positions." *NOW, WITH MY PATENTED INVENTIONS, I CAN PROVE THESE METHODS TO YOU.*

Q. Why do you use the words We, Us, and Our, instead of I or Me?

A. As you read through this book, you will see the use of these words interchangeably. This will make my truths unquestionable. Instead of one person verifying these methods, I have demonstrated them to others, and they support these STATEMENTS OF FACTS (not theories).

Q.   Do you believe that most people have a talent for baseball?

A.   Yes. If a person likes to watch or coach baseball, no matter what the age, he/she can play baseball. If the player is willing to practice just a few minutes a day, he/she can become a better than average baseball hitter. The secret to success in any sport is practice and more practice. But *THE BATTER MUST PRACTICE IN THE PROPER WAY TO IMPROVE. WITH MY DEVICES AND PATENTED INVENTIONS, THE BATTER WILL NOTICE THE DIFFERENCE VERY QUICKLY IN HOW HIS/HER HITTING HAS GREATLY IMPROVED.*

Q.   What is your opinion of the natural athlete?

A.   We do not believe that any person is natural at anything. Anyone has an equal chance, unless there is a health or physical disability. But even then, we believe with practice the player can be competitive. The player must read and practice, and then read and practice again and again to become a champion at anything. Now, if the player shows a certain athletic ability in high school, then a professional coach can take the player aside and teach him/her the proper way of running, jumping, etc. Even today, most of our top athletes in high school have had some professional instruction to help him/her become that champion. No person is going to just pick up a tennis racket, basketball, or golf club and be the best in that sport without proper instruction from a parent, coach or friend.

Q.   Why do you go over certain things in the book various times?

A.   We want the batter to fully understand the STATEMENTS OF FACT as he/she reads this book. And if someone should say to that batter, "That is wrong," he/she should reply, *"PROVE IT!"* WE EXPLAIN THINGS IN DIFFERENT WAYS. THAT WAY, THE BATTER WILL FULLY UNDERSTAND MY STATEMENTS OF FACT. If a batter, coach or reader says, "I do not understand," then just keep reading and looking at the pictures. It will become very clear. We do not want to hear any excuses of why the batter cannot hit the ball, no matter who the pitcher may be.

Q.   Is this recreational baseball book really going to make me a champion?

A.   We believe that if a batter wants to be a champion in baseball, this is the only baseball book that will instruct him/her properly. Also, we give the batter the reasons for hitting in a certain way. In addition, we show how to construct the simple baseball devices required for proper practice and attaining total improvement. No other baseball book does this.

Q.   What can you tell us about your inventions?

A.   I have developed the best devices for practicing baseball alone for total improvement. Somebody had to take the first step in advancing baseball. I feel this is what I have done. Remember, the first car was not a Ferrari, the first airplane was not a Mark IV jet, and the first telephone was not a cell phone. So, as you look at these inventions, don't ask, "What is the big sensation?" Try to look for my competition. After you read this book, you will know that there are no better inventions than mine, at this time or any other time, in the history of baseball. Thank goodness it was an American who wrote this baseball book.

Q.   Why are these batting apparatuses and patented baseball inventions so important?

A.   In tennis, we can practice on a backboard. In golf, we can go to the putting range and practice the swing. In boxing, we can utilize a punching bag. And so on. But in baseball, it's different. There are expensive pitching machines where the batter can pay money to practice. Or, he/she can buy some type of batting device which is worthless, because there are no instructions on how to hit the ball properly. *HOW CAN ANY BODY INVENT SOMETHING IF THEY DO NOT KNOW IT WORKS OR HOW TO USE IT PROPERLY*? I am giving *THE BASEBALL HITTER THE BEST DEVICES EVER CONCEIVED TO HELP HIM/HER WITH HITTING*. Also, this is the only book that describes how to use these apparatuses properly. This ensures the batter can practice alone to become a champion in baseball (if that is his/her desire). I have worked many years (along with God's help) to show what our baseball batters are doing wrong. I can "prove it" with these devices! By performing the exercises in this book, the batter will improve to unlimited ability. And the only person he/she will need is himself/herself.

Q. Did you show other people this method of hitting?

A. Yes. This will make my *FACTS* more positive. Instead of one person seeing these procedures, I have shown them to others, and they agree. Just as the player will agree with these FACTS (not theories), as they are explained along with my patented inventions.

Q. Is your method of hitting Fast Pitch Baseball the same as Easy Pitch Baseball?

A. Yes. The two methods will be similar, but with a small change in the timing of the swing and getting the proper picture or image in the batter's mind. The image for Slow Pitch and Fast Pitch will be different.

Q. What do you mean by the proper picture or image in the batter's mind?

A. I have made it possible for a batter to go from Slow Pitch Baseball to Fast Pitch Baseball without changing his/her style of hitting. Each invention puts a picture or image in the batter's mind as to when he/she will start swinging the bat. All the batter has to do is change baseball inventions for each type of baseball game. For example, in Fast Pitch Baseball, use the Bat Master; and in Slow Pitch Baseball, use the Easy Pitch Bat Master 1. Each type of baseball game will give the batter the proper image so as to hit the baseball for a home run. All the batter needs is the proper picture in his/her mind for each game, without changing batting styles.

Q. Are the pictures in the book on the Tee Master or Bat Master for Fast Pitch Baseball?

A. Yes. When using the Tee Master or Bat Master, the batter can only use this method.

Q. What do you mean?

A. Remember, the Tee Master is the same as the Bat Master, except the Tee Master has no Stance and Stride Device. They both have the similar positions at the plate when the ball is pitched. Notice the "*Hit Area*" of the bat on the ball when using the Tee Master/Bat Master. This is the only spot for each pitched ball, but the Bat Master is exactly right. Follow the book through each phase you are taught. For example, the first level addresses the use of the Stance and Stride Device. The second level helps to perfect the use of the Tee Master. The third level perfects the use of the Bat Master. Each phase will take time to perfect. So follow the book as instructed for total improvement. (Use this as a guide.)

Q.   What if the batter wants to keep his/her batting style no matter what you say?

A.   I am only giving the batter the basic foundation needed to improve hitting. Sure, I think the batter might make some "wee" changes (whatever that may be), because no two people hit "exactly" the same way. We are all different. But, the batter must have the correct foundation if he/she ever wants to improve. If the batter does not want to change his/her batting style, that is all right with us. So let us warn the batter: "We had to leave no stone unturned to prove my STATEMENTS OF FACT." If the batter thinks he/she has a good batting average now, he/she will find that, eventually, his/her batting average will surely drop if the batter does not use these instructions on hitting. This is what we're saying: "It's time for a change in hitting habits and the batter doesn't have any choice in the way I instruct." Therefore, if the batter still wants to keep his/her present batting style, then the reply is, "Good Luck! Be a champ, not a chump."

Q.   How do you know that your theory is correct on hitting?

A.   This is not a theory or guessing. When you have a device or invention, that changes theories into facts. You can see that for yourself when you use the Bat Master or Easy Pitch Master 1. *THAT IS WHY I AM CHALLENGING ANY PERSON, OR GROUP OF PERSONS, TO CHANGE THE STATEMENTS OF FACT IF THEY DO NOT AGREE.* To do this, he/she will have to invent something that will disprove my facts on Hitting, Throwing, Fielding, Base

Sliding, and Easy Pitch Baseball. First, they would have to write a baseball book to prove that they know something about baseball. Second, they would have to get a patent on the inventions as I did, so that they can prove they were first and that their facts are correct. Third, the invention would have to show that my inventions are wrong. At that point, I will sit down and talk baseball on who is right. It has been more than 150 years and no one has made this challenge. In 1845, Mr. Cartright and his staff wrote the rules on baseball. Who has done the rest? Who is the inventor of baseball? Where is his/her baseball book? Where are his/her inventions on Hitting, Throwing, Base Positions and Base Sliding? Where is his/her book on Slow Pitch Baseball and the patented inventions to prove his/her STATEMENTS OF FACT? Inventions must have instructions to show progress. Let's quit guessing and talk facts about baseball.

Q.   What was Winston Sports Trainers?

A.   It was a name I used to experiment and test my inventions.

Q.   How do you expect to see baseball played after all of your methods are learned to their highest level?

A.   When the player has learned all the hitting, throwing, outfield, infield and base sliding, then he/she will be a Master Baseball Player. In the game of baseball with Master Players, the rules will be the same, except the batter will get 2 balls and 1 strike, not 4 balls and 3 strikes. When you reach that level of baseball, you will be the best. *NOW THAT'S BASEBALL!*

Q.   How do you suggest I read this book?

A.   As you read each question, believe that the answer is correct. We recommend that the player put away his/her baseball bat and glove until he/she reads the book cover to cover, no matter how the player is hitting, throwing, playing outfield or playing infield. Presently, he/she is doing something wrong. What we're saying is, "THE PLAYER IS PERFECTING BAD HABITS; AND HABITS ARE DIFFICULT TO BREAK. THEREFORE, BE PATIENT WHEN YOU READ THIS BOOK." It has taken 40 years of very hard work and experimentation to ensure that the player is getting the proper knowledge. So, he/she can take at least a week or two, depending on time constraints, to read this book, knowing that it contains the knowledge to overcome the fear of facing a pitcher. But no matter which way the player chooses to practice, by using my patented inventions he/she must believe that he/she can become a CHAMPION IN THE ART AND SCIENCE OF BASEBALL.

ABOUT THE AUTHOR

When I was in the fifth grade, baseball became my favorite sport. In ninth grade, even though baseball was still my favorite sport, I was forced to choose between playing baseball and tennis. Because both sports were played during the same season in high school, I elected to play tennis. As much as I loved baseball, hitting the ball was very difficult for me. It was very discouraging to practice hour after hour, day after day, and still strikeout time after time. It seemed to me that the more I played baseball, the more my striking out prevailed. To be sure, there were many books about baseball that were available at the public library. But they were difficult to understand and the authors seemed unable to substantiate their theories.

On the other hand, the "how-to-play" books on tennis were simply written and easy to comprehend. Therefore, the sport of tennis was easier for me to grasp. In addition, I was able to practice tennis by myself, as well as benefiting from private instruction. Singular practice and private instruction are more difficult to obtain in a team sport like baseball.

As a result of my experience in tennis during my freshman year at high school, my ranking in Southern California was number 24 in the age 15 and under group. Also, in my freshman year, I was ranked number three on the tennis ladder, with only two seniors above me. During my sophomore through senior years, I was ranked number one. I was also league champion for three years; a four-year varsity letterman; and won many tennis tournaments. As I reflect on this, it doesn't seem too bad for someone whose real obsession was with baseball.

I enjoyed tennis very much, but I loved baseball. Throughout school, I wondered, "Why is my tennis ability so outstanding, while my performance in baseball so awkward and mediocre?" After high school, I began in earnest to find the answer to that question. I read every available book on the sport of baseball, and then studied everything I could find that related to baseball—from Little League, to semi-pro, to pro-games. I studied the characteristics of each player: the way each one hit; the way each one threw the ball; and analyzed the respective positions on the team.

Sometime later, while I was working as a locomotive engineer, I was given the opportunity to coach a baseball team. During that time, it became apparent that when you try a new concept in an old sport, no one listens. This is why it took the next 40 years to demonstrate beyond any doubt that my STATEMENTS OF FACT (as I call them) are correct.

It also bothers me that the only thing that seems important to most coaches is winning the game. There is a reason for this. Their jobs often depend upon having a "winning" team. As a result, coaches are always under a great deal of pressure. They may not have the time to teach, or they do not know how to teach. One coach told me, "We don't have the time to learn new ideas. We only have time to pick the best players and go out and win." Another coach said, "You have to be born with the ability to hit; no one can teach you." In my opinion, both of these statements are false.

Winning is great, but if you have a player who is good at throwing and poor at hitting, there is no reason to put that person on the bench, so long as he/she is willing to learn how to play baseball. For example, I would recommend that coaches help players put into practice the STATEMENTS OF FACT in this book. If a player can apply the basic principles outlined in this book, he/she can learn the art of hitting.

I am thoroughly convinced that when someone practices every day and still does not improve, the person is doing something wrong. Most likely, they are merely repeating and perfecting bad habits. This is precisely why I decided to write this book. The methods you will read about in the following pages are designed to correct the mistakes of coaches who have allowed hitters to continue incorrect methods of hitting. These incorrect methods cannot easily be corrected once they are learned, so I decided to write a book that would help baseball players and their coaches.

My intention is to educate ball players and spectators alike using a step-by-step method of learning all the important phases of how to hit a baseball. My statements are based on the premise that anyone who is willing to learn can become, if not a superior athlete, at least a better than average hitter. In this book, using a dialogue process of questions and answers, the player will learn many facets of baseball and will know what he/she is doing wrong so that the mistakes can be corrected. Also, using this question and answer technique, the reader can educate a friend or instruct a child in the art and science of hitting, throwing, fielding and base position. I will show many techniques, but in each instance only one technique is correct, and the patented inventions I have developed will prove it.

For instance, if the batter does not believe in my hitting method, take the pitcher aside and indicate what to throw to the batter in order to handicap his/her style of hitting. For example, if the batter's stride is more than seven inches and his/her knees are bent, the pitcher should throw the ball high and inside; the pitcher should never throw a low pitch. The techniques are intended to be helpful to both the offensive and defensive player, as well as the coach.

It takes at least three people to work with the batter when he/she practices hitting; otherwise, the batter will need to do a lot of walking or spend some money to go to a pitching machine. That is why my inventions (Bat Master, Bat Speed Apparatus, Backstop Master, etc.) are so important. Using them, the player can practice alone, and when diligent enough, he/she will be enabled to become a champion.

In order to achieve success in any sport, one must be able to practice alone using a good instructional method or guide. This book is such a guide. It is an excellent way for a player to improve in the sport of baseball. In order to become a champion in any sport, one is required to exercise, and then exercise some more. But training correctly is the foundation of becoming a champion. I always say, "To practice is the secret to being a winner, but practicing correctly is the secret to being a champion." By working with this book, using my patented inventions, and doing the exercises, you too can be a champion in the art and science of hitting, throwing, and base position.

When I first decided to write this book, my first task was to put my ideas into writing, to make these ideas simple and comprehensive for anyone who has an interest in baseball. It was difficult for me to explain each individual technique using words alone. Therefore, I had to become a photographer as well. I have taken all the pictures in this book in order to help me explain my methods to the baseball player, coach, and spectator.

In order to change my ideas into facts, I also needed a device or invention—a way to measure and record the results of the techniques I provided. Therefore, I had to become a draftsman. I had to draft these inventions in such a way that the players could construct their own devices at home. After becoming a draftsman, I became a designer. That was necessary because the designs were not fully correct at first; some changes needed to be made. Then, I had to test the invention for proper support, wear and tear, and make appropriate decisions, such as whether to use plastic, steel pipe, or both.

Next, I had to become an inventor. With each invention, I changed my "theories" into "facts." I have invented 19 baseball apparatuses for hitting, throwing, infield, outfield, base sliding, and Slow Pitch; designed 27 batting tees; 6 home bases, pitcher's plate; 8 sets of unique bases; and a backstop and batting cage. All can be made at home with a plastic pipe cutter or hack saw, pliers, screwdriver, tape measure and PVC glue.

Now, having combined these professions—instructor, author, photographer, draftsman and inventor—with 40 years of research and experience, I feel confident about what I have to say. During this time, I have specialized in only one thing: baseball. With my inventions, two patents, and hitting methods, I anticipate being able to some day virtually eliminate striking out and help players develop a more dynamic American Baseball Team.

Over the years, I have not been content to merely theorize or guess about how baseball could be improved. Instead, I persisted until I had developed a well-tested method in which I now have great confidence, one that has provided outstanding results. The teaching tools are my own inventions for enabling all baseball players to improve. Of course, there are many details in this process that must, of necessity, be left out of this introduction.

> FROM THE WHEEL TO THE SPACE SATELLITE, INVENTORS HAVE RECEIVED RECOGNITION FOR THEIR CONTRIBUTION TO PROGRESS. THEREFORE, LET THIS INVENTOR TEACH YOU—PLAYER, COACH, OR SPECTATOR—THE ART AND SCIENCE OF BASEBALL.

QUESTIONS

Q. *In hitting fast pitch and slow pitch baseball, at what point should the batter swing the bat to hit the inside, middle, and outside pitched ball?* Can **you** explain and **prove it** by demonstrating it with a device or invention?

Q. *How does the batter have Full Plate Coverage?* Can **you** explain and **prove it** by demonstrating it with a device or invention?

Q. *As a batter, are there any homemade devices or inventions that I can practice hitting by myself?* Can **you** explain and **prove it** by demonstrating it with a device or invention?

Q. *How can the batter hit a curve ball?* Can **you** explain and **prove it** by demonstrating it with a device or invention?

Q. *As a pitcher or fielder, are there any homemade devices or inventions that I can use to practice by myself for total improvement in throwing?* Can **you** explain and **prove it** by demonstrating it with a device or invention?

Q. *As a pitcher, what pitch should I throw to a batter who wiggles or moves the bat while at the plate?* Can **you** explain and **prove it** by demonstrating it with a device or invention?

Q. *Why do I hit pop-fly balls all the time?* Can **you** explain and **prove it** by demonstrating it with a device or invention?

Q. *Why can't I hit the ball properly in slow pitch?* Can **you** explain and **prove it** by demonstrating it with a device or invention?

Q. *Why do I swing late on the ball or hit the ball to the opposite field?* Can **you** explain and **prove it** by demonstrating it with a device or invention?

Q. *Why is it wrong for the batter to raise the rear arm in hitting?* Can **you** explain and **prove it** by demonstrating it with a device or invention?

ALL THESE QUESTIONS AND MANY MORE
WILL BE ANSWERED IN THIS BOOK.

HOW TO MASTER HITTING

1. *What is the purpose of this baseball book?*

    The purpose is to properly instruct any person, through a simple self-taught method, how to play baseball. It will explain the do's and don'ts of all base positions, throwing, fielding, hitting, and base stealing, as well as address the many more important segments of recreational baseball. Since the time the Americans who are recognized for developing baseball in 1845, baseball has not budged in progress for the batter. The old sayings, such as "Step into the ball," "Pitchers can't hit," "Simply, pick up a baseball bat and start swinging," "Just go out and practice" (even though there are no proper devices to practice with by yourself), or merely, "Keep your eye on the ball and swing the bat," among many others, will be something of the yesteryear in baseball. They will be replaced with new sayings for the future of baseball hitting, including "The batter must stride with the speed of the thrown ball, for if the batter's feet are incorrect, he/she will never hit the ball properly," "Swing the bat barrel ahead of the hands so the batter will not have a late swing when practicing with the Bat Master," and "Keep your eye on the ball when using the Bat Master, then the batter will have a picture in his/her mind of where the ball should be hit when he/she starts swinging the bat."

2. *Are you trying to get everyone to hit the same way?*

    Not exactly. But, by committing certain errors in hitting, such as over striding, making movements of all types, and not protecting the plate properly, the batter will never be able to hit accurately or with any amount of power. We want the player, spectator, and coach to understand that this book is an uncompromising, technological and educational baseball instructional book, which is easy to comprehend.

3. *How do we begin?*

With the step-by-step, assured self-taught techniques in this book. The player is going to learn every phase of recreational baseball, starting with the basics of hitting, throwing, fielding and base stealing, which most people know nothing about.

4. *What can you tell the batter about baseball bats?*

Always remember to keep the label of the bat in the up position. This way, the ball will not hit the label (wood bats only), one of the bat's weakest locations. Look for a bat with a large hitting barrel and a thin handle. If the handle doesn't seem thin enough, then scrape it down with a wood scraper or some type of tool that won't damage the wood of the bat. Then, use very rough sandpaper along the handle to give you better grip action. Apply some light wood oil and rub it in. DO THIS TO THE BAT ONLY IF YOU HAVE SHOPPED AROUND AND HAVE NOT BEEN ABLE TO FIND THE RIGHT BAT. If you find the correct bat, and if you have the money, you should buy an extra one just in case one breaks. Never lend your bat to anyone. When you are on a team, have your own special bat or bats. Keep your bat in its holder when not in use. Some teams may have a dozen baseball bats, but only one or two will be suited for you. If they break, you are out of luck. So, it's a good idea to have your own bat. Also, you should put your name or some mark of identification on your bat.

5. *What should the batter look for when picking a baseball bat?*

When picking a bat, choose one with as much wood in the "Hit Area" as you can find and as short as possible.

6. *What is the "Hit Area" of a baseball bat?*

The "Hit Area" of the bat is a seven-inch section starting two inches from the top of the bat and continuing down from there for seven inches. It is the part of the bat with which the batter will hit the ball. If the batter hits the ball on the end of the bat (first two inches), it will not go very far. If the batter hits the ball near the handle, it will sting the hands. The batter must hit in the "Hit Area" of the bat to get base hits and home runs.

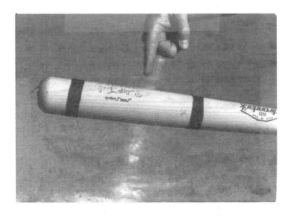

QUESTION # 6

7.   *Does the weight of the bat help the swing?*
> No. The batter wants a brief, strong swing, because that will decide the amount of power at the moment contact is made with the ball. Also, the *speed* at which the bat is swung is the important factor. The weight of the bat will not help the batter.

8.   *What will happen if the batter drills a hole in the end of the bat and fills it with cork?*
> The batter will take away the hitting power from the bat. If the batter removes the core of the bat and inserts cork, or any other type of material, it will be off balance.

9.   *What will happen if the batter cuts an inch off the end of the bat to make it shorter?*
> The bat will be improperly balanced. Never cut any amount of wood off the baseball bat.

10.   *What is one way the batter can learn to hit a baseball?*
> One way is to watch a great baseball player and attempt to imitate the player's batting style.

11.   *Is there another way?*
> Yes. The other way is to have a coach or friend look at your style of hitting and make the proper corrections, which you cannot see.

12. *Which of the two ways do you think is best?*

    Having a coach or friend teach a batter is best, because that person will watch the batter's style and can then correct the errors in his/her hitting style. But first, that person must read this book.

13. *Why can't I copy some famous baseball player?*

    You can, but you will want to develop your own style of hitting.

14. *What's the difference?*

    No two players have the same batting style. Once you understand the simple fundamentals of hitting, then you can build your own style of hitting.

15. *What is the first thing the batter should know about baseball and the hitting of the ball?*

    Learn the different types of pitches and how the baseball will react while in flight.

16. *How many basic pitches are there?*

    Three.

17. *What are they?*

    The fastball, curve ball, and change-up or slow pitch.

18. *What is the curve ball and how does it move when thrown by a right-handed pitcher?*

    The curve ball is a ball that moves and curves because of the spin the pitcher places on it. It will move in the direction of its spin. For a right-handed batter, the ball will curve away from him/her. For a left-handed batter, the curve ball will move toward him/her. The opposite is true for a left-handed pitcher.

19. *What is a slider pitch?*

    It is a modification of the fastball, but moves to the left when thrown by a right-handed pitcher. It will not have much of a curve to it.

20. *What is a knuckler or forkball pitch?*

    This is a slow pitch that will have a slow or gradual curve. It is also called a change-up pitch.

21. *What is the sinker pitch?*

    This is a fastball that drops, or goes straight down, just in front of the batter. Be careful of this pitch. It makes the batter over stride or lunge for the ball.

22. *What is a downer pitch?*

    This is a curve ball that comes straight at the batter, then drops straight down. A downer ball is a lot harder to hit than a wide curve ball.

23. *What is the screwball pitch?*

    This is a fastball that moves in toward a right-handed hitter when a right-handed pitcher is throwing the ball.

24. *What is a spitball?*

    This is also called power-ball or emery ball. It is illegal and has been banned from baseball. It is when the pitcher spits or applies something on the ball when he/she is about to throw it. REMEMBER, NO MATTER WHAT THE PITCHER THROWS, IT MUST BE IN THE STRIKE ZONE BEFORE YOU SWING THE BAT.

25. *What is a blooper pitch? (Used in underhand pitching only; discussed in later chapters.)*

    It is a slow pitch that the pitcher throws as slowly as possible and as high as possible. This was designed to throw the batter off stride or off balance. It will disturb the batter's timing and make him/her swing the bat too early.

26. *How does the batter hit the blooper pitch? (Easy Pitch Baseball.)*

    Do not try to over power the blooper. The batter must wait. This is discussed in a later chapter.

27. *What should the batter watch for on the blooper pitch?*

    The most important thing to watch out for is over striding. Do not over stride! It is very easy to do on this type of pitch, because the batter wants to go for the home run ball. Do as we just stated and the batter will get that home run ball—wait!

28. *What are the various types of deliveries a pitcher can throw?*

    They are: the underhand; the sidearm; the three-quarter style, and directly overhand.

29. *What about the underhand pitcher?*

    If the ball is thrown by an underhand pitcher, he/she will be able to throw a high fast ball or a high curve ball.

30. *What type of ball can't the underhand pitcher throw?*

    He/she will not be able to throw a low curve ball or a low fastball. All pitches thrown by an underhand pitcher will rise or go upward.

31. *What can you tell the batter about the sidearm pitcher?*
     The sidearm pitcher will be able to throw a wide curve ball
     that travels horizontally, on an even plane. As you bat
     and observe the sidearm pitcher, do not look at the way
     the ball is delivered. Concentrate on the ball. Do not take
     your eyes off the ball for even a second from the time it
     leaves the pitcher's hand until it is in the strike zone. Or,
     as some batters say, " . . . until the batter can see the
     ball leave the bat when hit upon impact." OF COURSE,
     THIS IS JUST AN EXPRESSION, NOT A FACT.

32. *What type of ball can't the sidearm pitcher throw?*
     The sidearm pitcher can't throw a "downer" or a "sinker"
     pitch.

33. *What about the three-quarter style pitcher?*
     This pitching style is the most difficult to hit against. The
     pitcher throws a sharp downer curve as well as an excellent
     fastball.

34. *What about the overhand pitcher?*
     It is not natural to throw directly overhand. This is an altered
     three-quarter style.

35. *What is the hardest pitch for most batters?*
     Any type of curve ball is the hardest pitch, especially the
     low outside curve ball. The reason is that batters do not
     want to get hit by the ball. We will discuss this type of
     pitch later in the book.

36. *What is the easiest pitch to hit?*
     The change-up or slow pitch is regarded as an easy pitch,
     but big league hitters do not like it because it throws them
     off stride and destroys their timing, which is adjusted to
     the speed of the pitch. Only those who are poor hitters
     seem to like this type of pitch.

37. *Is the curve ball an optical illusion?*
     Odd as it may seem, a lot of people believe that it is an
     optical illusion. Any hitter who has watched a curve ball
     will not agree. No, the curve ball is not an optical illusion.
     It is a dangerous ball that can destroy the batting average.
     In this book, we will give the batter the proper knowledge
     so he/she will know at some point how to handle the curve
     ball, as well as many other pitches.

38. *How can the batter tell what the pitcher is going to throw?*

Most youngsters do not properly cover the ball with their baseball glove; therefore, the ball can be seen. The batter should watch the covering of the ball. This takes practice, but once the batter gets the hang of it, he/she will know what we mean about calling which pitch is going to be thrown. When the batter sees the ball is not covered with the fingers, he/she can call a curve ball most of the time.

39. *What do most young pitchers throw?*

Most young pitchers will throw a majority of their pitches at full speed.

40. *What is the speed of the curve ball and fastball?*

The curve ball and fastball are thrown at about the same speed every time. Knowing this, the batter can stride or move the front foot faster.

41. *How about a slow curve ball?*

Now, for a pitcher who throws a slow curve or a medium fast curve, the batter does not need to stride the front foot as fast.

42. *Should the coach signal the batter on what the pitcher is going to throw?*

No. Most good hitters will study the opposing pitcher carefully before going to bat. They will attempt to figure out what type of ball the pitcher is throwing. Some league teams will have coaches at first and third who try to peak at the pitcher's grip on the ball in order to decide what will be thrown. The coach will then relay a signal to the batter. Some batters do not like to be told; others are glad to get this information.

43. *Is there a chance the coach could be wrong in the signaling?*

Yes, the coach might be wrong. The batter could get injured and lose all confidence in the coach. Good batters should do their own figuring and not depend on anyone else, because there is a chance of a mistake when signaling.

44. *Do pitchers try to fool the batters?*

Yes.

45. *What can the pitcher do to confuse the batter?*

Some pitchers will wind up slowly and throw a fast pitch. Others will wind up fast and then throw a slow pitch.

46.   *Which of the two pitchers is toughest to hit against?*

The batter will have a tougher time against a pitcher who always winds up the same way, but then varies the speed of the pitched ball. This is the pitcher with whom the batter will have his/her greatest troubles.

47.   *What should the batter look for on these pitchers?*

The only thing we can tell the batter to look at is the point of release, or the moment the ball is released by the pitcher. Then, keeping the hands and bat under control, the batter can hit any kind of pitch thrown, be it a fast curve or a slow ball.

48.   *What should the batter do if he/she gets nervous or tense at the plate?*

Before getting up to bat, the batter should take three deep breaths. While walking up to the plate, the batter has nothing to fear. Sometimes it helps to say a little prayer, such as "Lord, help me relax." Then, when in the batter's box, the batter should say to himself/herself, "I'm not scared of your weak pitches. The faster and more curve you (the pitcher) can put on the ball, the better I like it." Say this three times.

49.   *What will the pitcher do to make the batter nervous and tense?*

One of the things the pitcher will do is take a long time reading the catcher's signal. Then, the pitcher will wind up slowly and release the ball.

50.   *Is there anything the batter can do?*

Yes. If the batter feels the pitcher is taking too long, he/she can back out of the batter's box and tell the umpire that the pitcher is taking too long to throw the ball. Then, let the umpire decide. The pitcher has no right to play games with the batter, hoping to make him/her nervous or tense while at the plate.

51.   *Can the batter step out of the batter's box at any time?*

No. Once the pitcher starts his/her wind up to throw the ball, batter should not step out of the batter's box.

52.   *What should the batter do while waiting to enter the batter's box?*

If the batter is third or fourth in order to hit, he/she should practice on the Tee Master or Bat Master. When the batter is second or next to bat, he/she should observe the pitcher. Go to the batter's circle and try to judge the speed of the pitcher's throws. Get a side angle. Look at the delivery of the curve ball. Notice the delivery and see if the pitcher covers the ball all the time with the baseball glove. Finally, study the pitcher's position on the plate.

53. *What is so important about the pitcher's plate or rubber?*

The pitcher's plate or rubber is a full six inches wide and twenty-four inches long. There is nothing in the rules that says the pitcher has to pitch from the center of the rubber plate. He/she has the right to move to either side of the plate, whichever the pitcher prefers.

54. *Why would the pitcher want to move, let's say on the first base side of the pitcher's plate?*

Let's say the batter is right-handed. The batter will know before the first pitch is thrown that the pitcher is trying to make him/her nervous, or that the pitcher is angling so as to cross-fire the batter.

55. *Why would the pitcher do that?*

In that position, the pitcher is trying to make a fastball seem like a curve ball. Notice the pitcher's arms moving from his/her side. The batter will try to move away from the plate, stepping or striding down the third base line thinking he/she might get hit. Don't worry. Stay in there.

56. *What can the batter do to defend himself/herself?*

Call the umpire's attention to the pitcher's footwork on the mound. There is nothing more upsetting to a pitcher than having his/her footwork challenged. It makes the pitcher aware of his/her feet and not his/her arms.

57. *What good is there in telling the umpire?*

The pitcher's control and style may suffer. This is what the batter wants. Some might say that it is unfair for the batter to do that. They are wrong. The rules are very clear on how the pitcher should stand on and come off the plate. Let the umpire be the judge. That is one of the umpire's jobs.

58. *What is the strike zone of a baseball player?*

It is the width of the plate and the distance from the batter's knees to the armpits.

59. *Does it matter what size the batter is (referring to the strike zone)?*

> If the batter is a tall person, the strike zone will be longer. If the batter is a short person, the strike zone will be shorter. But the width is the same, seventeen inches.

60. *What of the illustration on the following page?*

> This illustration shows the strike zone of this batter. A pitch will not be a strike unless it is thrown inside the strike area, or Strike Master Jr. Sometimes, balls thrown outside the strike zone, or below the knees, are called strikes. You should remember that the umpires are human too and they sometimes make mistakes. The batter should never get angry with the umpire if he/she miscalls a pitch. If the batter wishes, he/she can remind the umpire without raising his/her voice. Be a gentle person. The umpire can throw a batter out of the game for being unruly. If that happens, he/she is no good to the team.

61. *Does being small make a difference in baseball?*

> Some think so. But, in our opinion, size does not mean a thing. The strike zone gives us all a fair chance. Some of our truly greatest stars were small persons, and this will continue. Under no circumstance, let your size stop you from playing baseball. That is why I wrote this baseball book. It is for the poor hitter, big or small, fat or thin. We all love baseball.

62. *What is the rectangle in the picture on the following page?*

> The rectangle is the strike zone for this batter. If the pitcher is good, he/she will try to throw the ball to the outer most corners of the rectangle. As pictured, they are: (1) the upper left-hand corner for outside high pitches; (2) the lower left-hand corner for low outside pitches; (3) the upper right-hand corner for high inside pitches; and (4) the lower right-hand corner for low inside pitches. This is for a right-handed batter.

63. *Do they have a name for these corners?*

> In baseball, these corners are called "spots." If you are a pitcher, you should practice throwing to these spots. The Device (SSMJC)

QUESTION # 62

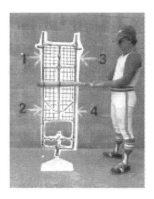

64. *What types of pitches can be thrown in the strike zone?*
    No matter what the pitcher throws, it must come into the strike zone to be a strike. So, as the batter stands at the plate, he/she should say to himself/herself, "Throw any type of pitch you want, just get it into the strike zone so I can hit the ball for a home run." (That is, unless the coach gives you the bunt sign.)

65. *Explain all you know about the distance the batter should stand away from the plate to get full plate coverage. (Using Stance & Stride Device)*

QUESTION # 65

It was difficult to show plate coverage until we worked with the Tee Master/Bat Master (this will be explained later). Most young batters persist in getting too close to the plate. In doing so, they only cover a portion of the plate. The Tee Master/Bat Master gave us a guide to show boys and girls how to attain full plate coverage. The batter must extend the arms full length, placing the "Hit Area"—or the end of the bat—two inches beyond the outside corner of the plate. You can see the batter is fully covering the plate. The batter has the proper distance from the plate to cover all parts of the plate. He is not too close to the plate and does not need to worry about inside pitches. Also, take a look at his front hip. It is opened a little bit. This way, he can hit inside pitches out in front by moving his front hip out of the way. He is not bothered with inside or outside pitches. He is using the Stance & Stride Device.

66. *What if the batter has longer arms?*

If the batter has longer arms or a longer bat, he/she should stand farther away from the plate.

67. *Do pitchers study the way batters stand at the plate?*

Sometimes, we wonder if they do. If they do not, they are poor pitchers. There are some major league batters who cannot reach outside balls within the "Hit Area" of the bat.

68. *Why can't some batters reach the outside pitch?*

They stand too far away from the plate in an effort to hit inside balls more effectively. Being aware of this, the pitcher just throws outside balls where the batter cannot reach them or will hit the ball on the end of the bat.

69. *How about the batter who stands too close to the plate?*

Batters who stand too close to the plate cannot get the "Hit Area" of the bat far enough in front to hit inside ball well. The batter will hit the ball on the handle of the bat and sometimes get a sting from the impact with the ball.

70. *Do pitchers study how the batter strides and where he/she hits the ball?*

Yes. Once the pitcher finds the weakness of the batter, he/she just throws to those spots.

71. *Can hitters make their own strike zone?*

    The rule book does not cover this very well, but umpires say: "If a batter is in the squat position while at the plate, then that will be his/her strike zone."

72. *Can the batter squat down low while at the plate?*

    Yes. The batter can get down as low as he/she wants, but the batter cannot change how wide the plate is. If the batter goes up to the plate, stands up straight, and then decides to squat down, the batter will have to take what the umpire calls.

73. *Can the batter try to fool the umpire?*

    Do not try to fool the umpire! More times than not, he/she will call a strike when it was a ball. Just go up to the plate and act naturally.

74. *What does over striding do to the batter strike zone?*

    Remember, all over striders seem to dip the front shoulder as they stride, making the strike zone lower than when they are in a normal batting position. The batter should not over stride, bend the front keens, or dip the shoulder. The batter will be judged on how he/she stands at the plate regularly and nothing else.

75. *What about holes dug in the ground from the previous batters?*

    Sometimes, there might be holes dug by the previous batters. In that case, call time out to the umpire and work out the area that fits your stance and stride.

76. *What is the size of the batter's box?*

    The batter's box is six inches away from the plate. It is four feet wide and six feet long.

77. *What if the batter is closer than six inches to the plate?*

    The batter is in an illegal position if he/she is any closer than six inches to the plate. That's why the Stance and Stride Device is so important. It keeps the batter at the proper distance from the plate.

78. *What is the reason for the six inches?*

    The six-inch distance was established because the Official Rules Committee did not want batters getting hit with the baseball. Remember, the batter should not prohibit the pitcher from throwing into the strike zone.

79. *Can the batter put his/her head over the plate when at bat?*
    No, the batter cannot put the head or knees over the plate.
80. *What's the first thing the hitter should do when he/she walks into the batter's box?*
    As soon as the batter walks into the batter's box, he/she should get into position for full plate coverage.
81. *When can the hitter walk out of the batter's box?*
    The hitter should not walk out of the batter's box unless he/she thinks the pitcher is trying to prolong the baseball game. If the pitcher does make the batter wait, just put the bat on the shoulder and wait. Then, when the batter gets ready to swing the bat, he/she should get back into the proper position.
82. *Should the batter get a tight hold on the baseball bat?*
    Yes, get a tight grip on the baseball bat just before the pitcher winds up.
83. *What should the batter do after getting full plate coverage?*
    Once the batter gets proper plate coverage, put the head up and get a mental picture of the strike zone. If you have been using the Tee Master/Bat Master, this should not be difficult. Also, don't forget to keep both eyes on the ball.
84. *How does the batter hit the ball?*
    The batter hits the ball with stance and stride.
85. *What is the batter's stance?*
    Some people say, "Just walk up to the plate and swing the bat." That sounds fine to a person who does not know anything about baseball. But remember, stance and stride are more important than anything. If the batter's stance and stride are off, he/she can never hit the ball properly. Notice the batter on the page. He is a right-handed batter. Both legs are straight (not bent). His back (right) foot is in a straight line. His front (left) foot is open a little bit, at about a forty-five-degree angle. The angle of his front foot in this position opens in the direction of the pitcher.
86. *Is this better than having both feet too close together or too far apart?*
    Yes.

87.   What is the secret of a good stance?

QUESTION # 85   QUESTION # 87, 88, 93

The secret of a good stance is to keep the right foot (rear foot) in a straight line and the left foot (front foot) at a forty-five-degree angle (for a right-handed batter). Using Stance & Stride Device.

88.   What is so good about this stance?

This stance is good because it provides for good balance and allows the batter to keep both eyes on the pitcher.

89.   What if the batter puts the feet close together?

If the batter brings the feet closer together, he/she is keeping only one eye on the pitcher. The batter will have to turn the head fully around to keep both eyes on the pitcher. Plus, the batter's weight will not be evenly distributed and cause him/her to be off balance.

QUESTION # 89 (WRONG)   QUESTION # 90 (WRONG)

90. *What if the batter opens the stance by putting the front foot toward third base? (Right-handed batter.)*

If the batter opens up the stance, he/she won't be able to hit the ball correctly to right field.

91. *Where will the batter hit the ball?*

Most of the batter's balls will go down the third base line. This will tell the team where to position for the batter. If the batter moves or strides the front foot toward third base, all the pitcher has to do is throw a good curve ball.

92. *What if the batter puts the front foot toward first base? (Notice picture.)*

If the batter moves the front foot toward first base, he/she won't be able to hit inside balls.

93. *What should the batter remember about the stance?*

Just remember to have the weight evenly distributed and to keep the knees straight. Also, remember to step in a straight line with the front foot at a forty-five-degree angle.

QUESTION # 92 (WRONG)   QUESTION # 94 (WRONG)

QUESTION # 95 (WRONG)

94. *What happens if the batter bends the front leg? (Notice Picture.)*
    If the batter bends the front leg, he/she will lose power and will not hit the ball hard. KEEP THE FRONT LEG STIFF.

95. *What happens if the batter widens the angle of the front foot? (Notice Picture.)*
    Some feel that widening the front foot toward the pitcher will allow them to hit the ball better out in front of them. But watch out. When the batter does this, he/she will have a tendency to step down the third base line. This refers to right-handed batters.

96. *What if the batter is left-handed?*
    For a left-handed batter, he/she would step down the first base line.

97. *Why do some batters hit only to one field?*
    Sometimes, the batter may be unable to keep a forty-five-degree angle on the front foot. So, when the batter opens up the stance, he/she will only be able to hit to one field. Do not try to use a stance that allows the batter to hit to only one field. Use the one shown by the model and he/she can cover all pitches—high, low, fast or slow.

98. *Tell me just what is the stride?*
    After the pitcher throws the ball, the batter must step and swing at about the same time if the pitch is one he/she wants to hit. It doesn't matter whether the batter steps a few inches (most good hitters step seven inches) or a couple of feet (like most of the poor hitters).

99. *Does the batter hit with the stride? (Using Stance & Stride Device)*

QUESTION # 98-102, 120

No. Nor does the batter hit the ball with the weight that he/she moves into the stride. But unless the batter strides properly, he/she will never hit the ball. Remember, the only thing the stride can do is place the batter into position to hit the ball. Construct the Stance and Striding Device, which is at the end of the chapter, and do the same as the pictures. Then go and practice.

100. *What is controlled striding?*

It means that every time the batter strides, he/she should step the same distance. If the pitcher throws the batter a slow ball, don't stride two inches. The proper striding or controlled striding is seven inches, and no more. Do what the model is doing until it becomes automatic and you can do it without thinking.

101. *How does the batter improve the stride?*

Do this in front of a mirror. Put the bat away. Place the hands just above the hips and make believe you are going to hit the ball. Then, all you should be thinking about is just striding. Remember, step with the speed of the pitched ball.

102. *What is the main purpose of the stride?*

With the stride, the batter is trying to place his/her power in the proper position in order to hit the baseball for a home run. The stride is mainly used for putting the batter in position, so that he/she can properly hit the ball.

103. *Why can't the batter stand at the plate, hold the bat steady, put both feet flat on the ground, and just punch the ball?*

No batter can be a flatfooted (no stride) hitter. What person can hit a home run standing flatfooted?

104. *Why does the batter have to stride?*

If the batter does not stride, he/she will not have the extra power that is required to hit a home run. The person who does not stride is scared of making a mistake, hoping to reduce all errors at the plate. This is not possible. The batter has to make a decision and not worry about the mistakes in striding.

105. *What is the batter doing in the picture?*

As the pitcher throws the ball, notice that the model prepares to step. The speed of the throw determines how fast he is going to step. As you will notice, he straightened his front leg just when he took his step.

This was to prevent him from losing his power when he hit the ball. The model's front leg is fairly straight. Do not try to hit with a bent front knee. If you do try it, notice how you lose all your power. Remember to stride seven inches all the time. Also, notice that the forty-five-degree angle is still on the front foot, just like when it was in the stance position and the rear foot has pivoted around and is on the toe of the foot. While doing this, be careful not to drag the rear foot.

QUESTION # 105

106. *What happens if the batter under strides?*
    The batter will hit the ball late if he/she strides five inches or less.
107. *What happens if the batter over strides?*
    Over striding is the worst of all. The batter cannot hit the ball hard. It also throws him/her out of position. If the batter strides eight inches or more, he/she is over striding.
108. *What is meant by "hitting off the heels?"*
    When using the controlled stride, the batter steps with the speed of the ball. Thus, he/she will never be guilty of this. "Hitting off the heels" means that the hips have begun to move away from the plate as the ball advances, and the batter ends up hitting the ball off the heels. In swinging the bat correctly, the batter should have a controlled stride. Then, the batter won't make the mistake of "hitting off the heels."

109. *Explain the expression "stepping into the ball."*

This phrase should never have been mentioned in baseball. It is the worst enemy to any ball player. If you hear someone say it, correct him or her. Tell them the batter should never step into the ball. That is why the pitcher has such an extreme advantage over the batter. What the person means to say is, "The batter strides with the speed of the ball." You, as the batter, are then in complete control.

110. *What do you mean when you say, "stride with the speed of the ball?"*

What we mean by this is that the batter uses the front foot, the foot the batter strides with, as a guide so he/she can calculate the speed of the pitched ball. If the pitcher is a fast pitcher, stride fast. If the pitcher is a slow pitcher, slow the stride down. Once the batter has mastered this technique, he/she will have acquired a necessary and most important trait for hitting. But remember, seven inches when striding. Also, along with the stride, use the eyes and hands in conjunction when hitting the ball.

111. *How would the pitcher throw to a very fast strider?*

The pitcher should give the batter a slow pitch and watch him/her hit a weak ground ball or pop-up (hit the ball high in the air) to the infielders.

112. *What should the batter do to avoid getting hit by the ball?*

We know it is hard, but try not to be scared of being hit by the ball. The batter should check his/her distance from the plate to get full plate coverage. Use the Tee Master/Bat Master to practice this. Learn to fall to the ground if a ball is coming toward the body or head. When practicing the stride, also practice turning the back and falling to the ground. It is better to get hit in the back than in the chest, stomach or even in the face. A ball that hits the front of a batter's body will hurt a lot more than the back. There is little pain if the batter is hit in the back.

113. *Can the batter put a hand up to stop the ball if it is coming at him/her?*

No. It is prohibited and the umpire could call a strike on the batter for that. If a batter practices falling to the ground when striding, he/she will not have to worry much about getting hit. Most batters who get hit are usually guilty of being too close to the plate, or they have not adequately practiced falling to the ground to avoid wild pitches.

114. *Is it possible for a left-handed batter to hit to the opposite field on an inside fastball or inside curve?*

It is possible, but the batter cannot do it effectively. There is no reason why a left-handed batter should want to hit to the opposite field. The coach can call a hit-and-run play with a left-handed batter at the plate. However, if the left-handed batter hits to left field (opposite field), the runner may not make it to third base. It is easier for a runner to be thrown out going from first going to third base by the left fielder than by the right fielder.

115. *How could the batter hit to the opposite field if he/she wanted to?*

The batter would have to move the front foot and make it mobile, moving it toward the opposite field he/she wanted to hit. The batter would also have to angle the bat.

116. *What is so hard about that?*

It takes less than two seconds for the ball to reach the plate after it leaves the pitcher's hand. That is not very much time to decide if it is going to be an outside, inside, high, or low pitch. Also, there isn't much time to move the foot.

117. *What do you suggest?*

Hit where the ball is going to be pitched. If it is outside, it will go to the opposite field. If it is inside, it will go to the left field for a right-handed batter. Now, this is what the batter should keep in mind: "THE FRONT FOOT SHOULD STRIDE IN A STRAIGHT LINE ALL THE TIME AND THE BATTER SHOULD NOT TRY TO MOBILIZE THE FRONT FOOT BECAUSE IT IS NOT NATURAL, NOR DOES THE BATTER HAVE THAT MUCH TIME."

118. *If the batter swings late, can he/she hit the inside ball to the opposite field?*

No matter how late the batter swings, he/she cannot hit a perfectly thrown inside ball to the other field. There is only one way the batter can do it, but it is not natural. If the batter is right-handed, he/she will have to angle the bat to left center field, place himself/herself far from the plate and step or stride toward the plate. Left-handed batters will have to do the opposite.

119. *Explain this idea again about the batter, except in more detail.*

As the batter stands at the plate, he/she hits the ball where it is pitched. A batter has no chance of hitting to the opposite field on an inside pitch; that is, with any type of conformity. The batter should hit the ball where it is going to be pitched if he/she strides identically the same way (straight ahead), have the proper plate coverage, and be sure to get the front hip out of the way.

120. *What does the inside ball have to do with the front hip?*

Let us say, "THE STRIDE ONLY PUTS THE BATTER IN POSITION TO HIT." If the batter does not move the front hip out of the way, he/she will not be able to hit inside

FRONT HIP **REAR HIP**

QUESTION # 120

balls effectively. The batter will miss the ball completely or hit the ball on the handle of the bat and get that stinging sensation. Go over and practice with the Stance and Striding Device again. This should be done in front of a mirror. Do not use a bat. Take and adjust the stance twelve to twenty inches on the Stance and Striding Device. Next, put the hands just above the hips, for the batter wants good balance and even weight distribution on both legs. Now, go practice until it becomes a normal reflex. Also, to make the stride and stance superbly accurate, move the front hip out of the way as you stride. Then you will have made considerable progress in becoming a CHAMPION IN THE ART AND SCIENCE OF HITTING.

121. *Explain what a shoulder twitch or jerk is.*

A shoulder twitch is when the batter, during his/her stride, pulls the bat and shoulder back toward the catcher while the ball is approaching. It destroys the rhythm and the batter will hit late on the ball. The batter will not be able to hit inside pitches between the belt and armpit.

122. *What is wrong with using a shoulder twitch?*

With the shoulder twitch, the batter cannot move the bat out in front of the plate quickly enough to get the "Hit Area" of the bat on the ball.

123. *Is it wrong to twitch at the plate when the batter is nervous?*

Yes. Twitches are hand jerks or movements indicating nervousness, or that the batter can't make the proper decision on hitting the ball. Twitches are something the batter does before he/she swings the bat. If they are not brought under control soon enough, twitches become handicaps. IT WILL NOT BE CALLED A TWITCH IF THE MOVEMENT DOES NOT OCCUR WHILE THE BALL IS IN FLIGHT, AND ABOUT TWENTY FEET AWAY FROM THE BATTER.

124. *Can twitches be corrected?*

Yes. If corrected at the proper time, they are just quirks that do not interrupt the swing of the bat while hitting the ball.

125. *What about the "foot hitch"?*

A "foot hitch" is lifting the front foot. The foot hitch occurs before the batter takes the stride.

126. *What about the moving of the baseball bat?*

Many hitters move the bat back and forth before the ball is pitched. Some do this to relieve tension at the plate, or because of nervousness. A smart pitcher could wind up slowly and wait for the bat to start wiggling, then throw the ball right past the batter.

127. *Can these twitches or hitches hurt the hitter's batting average?*

Yes. These defects in style could be very dangerous to a hitter's batting average. To have perfect hand control, the hitter cannot have any twitches or jerks.

128. *How should the batter hold the baseball bat?*

The bat should be held firmly so that it will not move from the line of the swing. With the ball coming at split-second speeds, it is most important that the bat not move or the batter's timing will be thrown off.

129. *Are hand twitches involved with this pinned arm idea?*

Yes. I cannot talk enough about twitches. Twitches are hand jerk motions. They indicate indecision or nervousness, something batters do before swinging the bat. If not checked in time, the batter will have a big handicap. The batter will not have perfect hand control if he/she has a hand twitch. Hold the bat firmly so that it will not sway from the line of the swing. When the ball is moving at split-second speeds, it is very important that the bat is motionless, because any movement will throw off the batter's timing.

130. *What if the batter hits foul balls a lot?*

More than likely, the batter has a shoulder twitch.

131. *What if the batter hits pop-up fly balls a lot?*

Again, the batter has a shoulder twitch. Don't forget, any type of twitch will make the batter swing late on the ball so he/she just gets a piece of the ball.

132. *What do they mean by "getting too far out in front of the ball?"*

The batter can lose a lot of his/her power by doing this. The batter will try and move the bat forward too fast, trying to make up for a late swing.

133. *Would the shoulder twitch have anything to do with "getting too far out in front of the ball?"*

Yes. As the batter strides, he/she will pull the bat and the shoulder in the direction of the catcher. There will be no rhythm. The batter will be late swinging at the ball. The batter will not be able to hit anything inside between the belt and armpit. Don't forget, with a shoulder twitch, the batter cannot move the bat out in front of the ball fast enough to get the "Hit Area" of the bat on the ball.

134. *Is fear at the plate a natural thing?*

Yes. But to overcome fear at the plate, the batter must have knowledge of hitting. If the batter does not know how to hit properly, he/she will be scared. It is my job to teach the batter so he/she will not be scared. It is a horrible thing to get up to the plate and swing the bat and not know what the batter is doing wrong. If it lasts long enough, the player will say the heck with baseball and go to some other sport. I don't blame people for getting angry at trying to hit the ball, but all sports take work, and more work. I have read a lot of books on baseball, but none of them tell the batter why he/she should bat a certain way and what happens if the batter does not follow the proper batting method. If a batter's average does not improve using my STATEMENTS OF FACT, then reread this book.

Obviously, the batter is doing something wrong hitting the ball. Keep reading the book until you can see your swing in your sleep, and then go out there and murder that ball.

135. *What's so different about this method?*

You will notice so far that the batter's legs must be straight, but the pinning of the batter's back arm against the body is the biggest argument.

136. *Explain the pinned arm idea.*

The theory now is to keep the batter's arms away from the body. This theory is completely wrong if the objective is for the batter to achieve greater power in his/her hitting. Notice the batter in the illustration on the page. The batter's front (left) arm (right-handed batter) is raised. This is for guiding the swing of the bat. So raise the front arm. Now, here is the big one: the batter's back arm is pinned up against the side of his body. This way, a batter can achieve greater driving power to put the ball over the fence.

137. *What about the model (refer picture No. 137)?*

The model is holding the bat loosely in his hands until the ball is ready to be pitched. Then he tightens the hands for power. The model has his left-hand knuckles facing up and his right-hand knuckles pointing back toward the catcher. Believe me, the timing is in those hands! Remember, the batter's hands are controlling the swing. Avoid letting the body or stride control the swing. Force the hands to do it.

138. *What is the "push motion with the hands?"*

The pinned right arm, the hip, the shoulders and the wrist snap combine for total power.

(CORRECT)
QUESTION # 136, 137

(WRONG)

But the real power is in the "push motion" that is generated as the right arm moves way from the body.

139. Can you give an example?

Yes. Put a bat in the right hand, pin the arm and swing. The batter can feel that he/she has more power in the

QUESTION # 138

right arm than in the left arm (right-handed batter). Therefore, the left arm should be more of a guide than the one with the most strength. To prove my point again, swing the bat fourteen inches using the snap of the wrist for strength. The batter will be surprised to see how the wrist can get a quick whip action. Make the swing in the fastest speed attainable in the shortest possible distance. Then the batter will have extra power as well as increased accuracy for the long hard hit ball.

140. What about the shoulders and the flight of the ball?

Each time the batter swings the bat, he/she should begin with the shoulders if the ball is pitched either high or low. Let's say the flight of the ball is low. The batter does not drop the baseball bat on the same flight level as the ball.

141. Why?

Because one way a batter hits fly balls or pops-up is when he/she gets into the routine of dropping the bat to the same level as the ball's flight.

142. If the batter doesn't drop the bat with the flight of the ball, then what is he/she doing?

This is what we are trying to do. It is from the line of the shoulders that we are attempting to hit the ball. With any balls pitched either high or low, the batter will swing the bat from the shoulder level. This will put the ball on that level of flight.

143. *What will that do to the flight of the ball?*

The ball will be hit like a line drive from the shoulders. If the ball is pitched in the middle or belt zone area, it will go at that height; if it is pitched low or near the knees, it will go on the ground. If it goes on the ground, there is a possible base hit. However, a low pitched ball will sometimes climb and go over the fence, the same as on a high pitched ball.

144. *What about a ball pitched below the knees?*

Use the vertical swing for balls below the knees. On the bat, the hitting zone is the same. On balls below the knees, the batter uses the vertical swing, holding it as long as he/she can, just like the model is doing. This will stop the batter from hitting the low balls into the air for pop-ups. Low balls are enjoyable only if the batter hits them properly. We do not think a batter will hit a ball this low, but it is possible. Use the Bat Master putting the height pole in FRONT OF THE MIDDLE SOCKET. (Refer chapter Bat-Master.)

145. *Is there such a thing as a "bad ball hitter?"*

There are some batters who like the ball pitched just inside, low, or just a bit outside. They are referred to as "bad ball hitters."

146. *How can the batter practice low pitched balls below the knees using the Vertical Swing (Refer to Picture No. 146, Steps #1 & #2)?*

QUESTION # 144, 146

To begin, the batter needs a reflective picture of how he/ she will appear in his/her own mind. The batter will not use a ball to start. Get in front of a mirror and mark a spot fourteen inches in front of the plate, or use the Tee Master/ Bat Master for more accuracy. Now, hold the bat along this imaginary line until you hit this mark of fourteen inches. Then snap your wrist and follow through. This is similar to a golf swing. Practice this swing a few minutes each day.

147. *What if the batter doesn't use the Three-Quarter Horizontal swing for low pitches?*

A pitcher once said, "There are only two pitches I want to perfect, the low fast ball inside for right-handed batters, and the low fast ball outside for left-handed batters." That is because there are very few hitters who use the three-quarter horizontal swing. I know that a low fastball or low curve ball will handicap most hitters unless they use the three-quarter horizontal swing.

148. *What else is important about the Vertical Swing for below the knees and the Three-Quarter Horizontal Swing at knee level?*

This is going to be a very big argument among baseball players who have been doing this all their life, but it is called pinning the right arm up against the body (right-handed batter). UNDER NO CIRCUMSTANCE SHOULD THE BATTER KEEP THE REAR ARM AWAY FROM THE BODY ON THE VERTICAL SWING OR ON ANY OTHER TYPE OF SWING. KEEP THE REAR ARM CLOSE TO THE BODY.

149. *Tell me again why the batter should press down the rear arm?*

First, the batter will lose a lot of his/her power by keeping the arm away from the body. When I made the Tee Master/Bat Master, I asked a batter to swing as hard as he could, first with the arm away from the body, and then with the arm pinned up against the body. The result was that the swing with the arm pined up against the body generated more power.

150. *Did the batter have any type of problem with the pinned arm method?*

Yes. Using the right arm as the one driving force, the only problem was that the batter had a habit of a "pulling type motion" so it made it difficult to hit to the opposite field.

151. *Did you find a way to cure that problem?*

Yes. With the Tee Master/Bat Master and the proper instructions that are contained in this baseball book, we cured that problem.

152. *How did you do it?*

If the batter extends the arms fully, and using a pushing motion with the right arm across the plate for pitches down the middle, outside balls, and inside balls, we found that with the Tee Master/Bat Master, we could teach rear arm action with all these pitches. We repeat, THERE IS MORE POWER IN THE REAR ARM, WITH THE ARM PINNED, THAN WHEN KEEPING IT AWAY FROM THE BODY.

153. *Does the wrist have any more power?*

Yes, the right wrist has twice as much whip action and more roll using the pinned arm method. (For right-handed batter; for left-handed batters, the left wrist.)

154. *What is the purpose of the Tee Master or Bat Master?*

It was designed to show the different types of hitting strikes. It also lets a person learn how to swing a bat properly.

155. *Why do you call them Tee Master and Bat Master?*

Because they are the only devices I can think of that will convince the batter that this is the best technique yet conceived for how to master the Art and Science of Hitting a Baseball. Use your old batting stance and it will convince you. The batter might be good on low balls but bad on high pitches. THE OBJECT IS TO MAINTAIN THE SAME TYPE OF BATTING POSITION ALL THE TIME, NOT TO MOVE THE STANCE DIFFERENT WAYS FOR DIFFERENT PITCHES. THE BATTER DOES NOT HAVE THE TIME WHEN THE BALL IS COMING AT SPLIT-SECOND SPEED.

156. *What should the batter do before he/she starts using the Tee Master/Bat Master?*

Try to get a reflective picture of what his/her strike zone should look like. The batter can stand at the plate all day and if he/she doesn't know what he/she should look like at the plate, the batter will never hit the ball very hard or even at all.

157. *How can I get this picture of myself and how to swing properly?*

Some of the top baseball players use the mirror. First, study the pictures in this book. Then, get a picture in your mind of how you should look. Finally, get in front of a mirror and practice. You can then check to see if you look the same as the pictures in this book.

158. *Why is it that most people who play baseball are such poor hitters?*

> Because in baseball, most batters are not taught the proper movement of the hips, hand control and striding. Most people just pick up a bat and start swinging. Some never practice because they do not have the proper devices to practice with or cannot find enough players. In addition, they can't find a pitcher who knows how to pitch strikes. But no matter how much the batter practices, if he/she continues making fundamental mistakes in timing, he/she will never hit the ball correctly. Also, some have no idea where the strike zone should be, or what they should be doing when trying to hit different types of pitches. That is the purpose of all my baseball inventions, to remove any excuse the baseball player has to practice. The only person he/she will need is himself/herself.

159. *When the ball is not moving, how does using the Tee Master/ Bat Master help the batter?*

> AT THE TIME THE BATTER HITS THE BALL, THE BALL IS NOT MOVING. THE BATTER WILL HAVE TO GET A PICTURE OF THE BALL MOVING AT SUCH A FAST SPEED. THE ONLY WAY IS TO STOP THE BALL. THAT IS WHY THE TEE MASTER/BAT MASTER IS SO IMPORTANT. IT STOPS THE BALL WHERE THE BATTER IS SUPPOSED TO HIT IT. THE BATTER'S MIND AND EYES PICK UP PICTURES AND RELAY THEM TO OTHER PARTS OF HIS/HER BODY. THE MORE THE BATTER USES THE TEE MASTER/BAT MASTER, THE STRONGER THE PICTURE.

160. *Will the Tee Master/Bat Master teach me hand control?*

> Yes. It will show the batter how valuable the hands are in hitting the ball.

161. *Can the Tee Master/Bat Master improve the batter's timing when hitting the ball?*

> Yes. It will improve their timing greatly.

162. *Will the Tee Master/Bat Master make the batter an accurate type hitter?*

> Yes. It will teach the batter how to be a lot more accurate in his/her hitting.

163. *Does the Tee Master/Bat Master show the batter how to have proper plate coverage?*

    Yes. It will teach the batter how to have the correct plate coverage.

164. *Can the Bat Master help the batter to get the appropriate stance at the plate?*

    Yes. It will give the batter the proper stance he/she needs for their hitting.

165. *Will the Tee Master/Bat Master improve the batter's coordination?*

    Yes. It will help the batter's coordination improve immensely.

166. *Can the Tee Master/Bat Master show the batter how to hit the various types of pitched balls?*

    Yes. It will show the batter how to hit the various types of pitched balls—high, low, inside, outside and anything in the strike zone.

167. *Will the Tee Master/Bat Master also show the batter how to use the hips correctly?*

    Yes. It will show the batter how to use his/her hips correctly.

168. *Can the Bat Master show the batter the correct distance he/she should stand from the plate?*

    Yes. It will give the correct distance the batter should stand from the plate.

169. *Will the Bat Master help the batter to use the controlled stride?*

    Yes. It will show the batter how to use the controlled stride correctly.

170. *Can the Tee Master/Bat Master improve the batter's concentration?*

    Yes. It will make the batter concentrate much better while at the plate.

171. *Will the Tee Master/Bat Master make the batter a lot stronger at hitting the ball?*

    Yes. The batter will be extra strong at his/her hitting.

172. *Some have asked, "Is it proper to hit a ball pitched down the middle to left field (right-handed batter)?"*

    The answer is no. When the batter is swinging the bat properly, it will go to left center field. If the batter's hands are moving slowly and his/her timing is incorrect, then the ball pitched down the middle will go to right field. That's why hand control is so important.

173. *Can you explain what you mean by "the speed of the bat in the strike area."*

Yes. First, using the Bat Speed Apparatus, the batter wants to place the ball over home plate (construction at end of chapter). Second, adjust the plate for an outside, middle or inside ball. Third, adjust the wire for high, middle, or low ball. Fourth, give the ball a light push and try to hit it with the bat—USE THE HANDS ONLY, DO NOT STRIDE OR ROTATE HIPS OR SHOULDERS. While the ball is moving, try and touch the ball without much force at first. Then, as you get better, increase the speed of the swing. Only with the Bat Speed Apparatus, as the batter hits the ball it will bounce off the tarpaulin and come back. For a faster return of the ball, place a large piece of wood in front of the tarpaulin. The ball will bounce off the wood and return quicker. USE IT LIKE A PADDLE BALL. Place the "Hit Area" of the bat on the ball as it returns (for extra strong wrists use a heavier baseball bat). With the controlled hands exercise, the batter will have the power to hold back on the thrown ball (in the last moment) to decide if the pitch will be a strike or a ball, before swinging the bat. We are trying to make the batter have CONTROLLED EXTRA-QUICK HANDS for hitting that ball for a home run.

174. *Is there a different way of explaining "Bat Speed?"*

No. We cannot think of any other way this "bat speed" works, except if the batter wants to construct a "Bat Speed Apparatus" in an easier way. In the garage, put an eye screw in one of the beams in the ceiling. Then, run the wire through the eye screw and the ball, tying a knot in the end of the ball. Use the same basic principles and instructions as above. With this type of device, the ball will not bounce back unless the batter puts something in front of the ball. Also, if the batter increases bat swing speed, the ball will go over the beam and get tangled-up. It is a substandard way of practicing this hand control exercise, but at least the batter is practicing. The thing that we must emphasize is that the batter must practice this hand control—it is very important and will prevent him/her from striking out at the plate. Even if the batter has to hang the ball from a tree, go out and practice, practice.

175. *Why is "Bat Speed" so important in the strike zone?*

If the batter wants to hit a long ball, then he/she cannot swing the bat slowly. What the hitter must have is "Bat Speed" in the strike zone. That is, the hitter must swing the bat as fast as possible in the strike zone area. When the batter can do this properly, then he/she will be able to obtain the power to hit a home run. The purpose of all this is that the faster the batter swings in the strike zone, the better he/she will hit the ball.

176. *How about if the batter swings the bat wild and fast?*

What the batter wants to do is have control of the bat at all times. A wild fast swing is not much good if the batter misses the ball. But a solid strike that the batter has under control with fast bat speed is what we want.

177. *How can the batter tell which arm is the stronger of the two arms?*

Place the ball on the Tee Master/Bat Master. Then use the right arm and hit the ball with the bat. Then use the left arm and hit the ball. Whichever arm hits the ball farther is the stronger arm. In this manner, the batter will be able to tell which arm is stronger.

178. *Which arm should be up against the body?*

The arm that is pinned up against the body is the stronger arm. If it does not seem so, then the hitter is batting wrong. Remember that the back arm is the one with all the power, not the front arm.

179. *What is the front arm (bent arm) used for?*

The front arm is used as a guide and for balance, nothing more.

180. *As the pitcher winds up, is pulling the bat back toward the catcher a bad habit?*

Well, if the batter does this, he/she will create a larger curve on the swing and increase the strike area. Remember, if the batter has good controlled hands, this will create a little more power. This pulling back motion should occur before the stride, not along with the stride. After the bat is pulled back and stopped, then the stride is made as the ball is thrown by the pitcher; otherwise, it will be a shoulder twitch. So there is no movement of the bat once the ball is in flight, or even better, no movement of the bat once the pitcher starts his/her wind up.

181. *Who would supply more power upon impact of the ball on the bat, the pitcher who throws the ball or the batter who swings the bat?*

We believe the batter would. We think the batter would supply more power, but we have no way of proving it.

182. *Is it true that the longer the batter can hold the baseball bat back, the greater the power?*

Yes, it is true. The batter will hit balls farther the longer he/she can hold back on the power, just before swinging the bat. This is sound advice because the ball is traveling at its highest speed upon impact with the bat.

183. *How is the bat moved into the strike area to make a proper swing?*

QUESTION # 183

(CORRECT)

QUESTION # 184   QUESTION # 185
(WRONG)

With the end of the bat moving in the direction of the ball, the batter will swing the bat with the hands acting as a pivot point. This is not as easy as it sounds. Remember, the hands have to act like a swivel moving the end of the bat toward the ball. As a matter of fact, this is the most complicated stage of the whole hitting procedure.

184. How do most batters swing the bat?

Almost all baseball players move their hands in front of the barrel of the bat into the strike area.

185. Is this wrong?

Yes. As the batter strides, it is almost a habit for the batter to move the hands ahead, with the hit zone end of the bat following behind. Now, for the batter to try to get the hit zone of the bat into the hitting position with the hands ahead of the bat, the batter will have to try to fling the bat through faster than he/she possibly can and with the hands ahead of the hit zone the hitter will have a late swing and a poorly hit ball.

186. Please explain, I do not understand.

What I am saying is, when the batter slices the ball or swings late and hits the ball to right field (opposite field), the batter's hands are moving ahead of the hit zone of the bat. Try to think of this as pertaining to the coverage of the plate. In the batter's strike zone he/she can hit any ball. The batter will always be out in front of the ball on the swing if he/she uses the hands like a swivel, and fling the hit zone of the bat toward the ball with the hands trailing behind. (Picture No. 183.)

187. Could the batter have any problems moving the bat toward the ball with the hands trailing behind?

Yes, the batter could. The only problem the batter might have to anticipate is attempting to hit the ball before the ball gets to him/her. Then the batter will have the tendency of moving the bat out in front too fast. The way the batter improves this alteration is by using the Tee Master/Bat Master and that involves practice and more practice.

188. Can you explain the whole thing to me another way?

Yes. When the batter begins the stride and moves the shoulders slowly while the ball is advancing, that bat makes a curve that covers the entire strike area. Now, the batter's hands act like a "swivel" that begins the curve and makes the bat move like a pendulum of a clock.

189. *What makes the curve in the batter's swing important?*

This is the faultless way to swing a baseball bat. Any other type method is wrong.

190. *Why must the hands act as a pivot point as pertaining to a pendulum of a clock?*

To give you an example of how the batter can lose a lot of his/her power, try the following. Step and move the shoulders forward. Now, notice the position of the baseball bat. It has fallen behind you. In that split second, the batter did not employ the hands to act like a swivel or the pivot point of a pendulum, and since the hands did not move the hit zone of the bat forward the hitting power is removed.

191. *Does the front hip have anything to do with the bat swing?*

Yes. When the batter steps and turns the shoulders, I want you to notice the front hip (hip farthest from the catcher) and how it moves out of the way instinctively, or just like a reflex. So, as the batter takes the stride and starts turning the shoulders, the bat will start moving into the strike zone. Watch the hip movement. (Picture No. 193, Step 2.)

192. *How can I practice using my hands like a swivel?*

When you practice using your hands like a swivel, set the ball on the Tee Master/Bat Master. Take your regular stance position, but with this exercise you will not stride. Stand there and slowly swing the hit zone of the bat forward in the direction of the ball with the hands falling behind. Having tried this a few times, you will regard this as an excellent way of having more power in the right hand.

193. *Explain the whole process of hitting, from the time the batter goes up to the plate until the batter hits the ball. (Picture No. 193.)*

When the batter walks up to the plate, he/she wants to check the batter's box to make sure there are no holes or dips in the batter's box from other players' use. If there are, take the spikes on the shoes and fill the holes or dips for the batter's type of stance. Make sure the batter calls time out while he/she does this. If the batter doesn't call time out, the pitcher can pitch the ball. (Step #1) As the

STEP # 1

STEP # 2

STEP # 3

STEP # 4

QUESTION # 193

batter gets into the batter's box, the stance should be about sixteen inches for this model. The legs should be straight, the bat should be resting on the shoulders, the front foot should be at a forty-five degree angle, and the rear foot should be in a straight line. Pinning the right rear arm (right-handed batter), the left arm is up in the air as a guide and for balance. The pitcher winds up. The batter takes the bat off the shoulders and gets a solid grip on the bat, not moving the bat at all. The pitcher throws the ball. (Step #2) Now, if the ball is slow, the batter takes the seven-inch stride according to the speed of the ball, using the stride as a guide. Moving the front hip out of the way (hip farthest away from the catcher), the batter stills has the bat held under control. As the batter is striding, the shoulders will start to move forward. Still keeping the bat under control, the batter decides whether he/she wants to hit the ball or not. Now, a lot of youngsters get too anxious and they stride and move the shoulders and hips too fast. In moving the bat into the strike area too soon, the batter will notice a loss of power. It will take some time for the batter to master this, but the more he/she practices, the easier it will become. (Step #3) The model has decided that this is the pitch he wants to hit. He has moved the bat forward, away from his body, with the hands behind the barrel of the bat, not in front. Also, look at his front leg. It is still straight. As is the rear leg. The legs are not bent at the knees. At the moment of impact, the batter snaps the back hip (hip closest to the catcher) into the swing at the same moment for that extra power. Now, the batter can lose the "hip snap" if he/she lets the rear leg or right leg bend at the knee, for this will create a dip and the hip snap motion is lost. So, by all means, keep the rear leg as straight as possible during the whole process of hitting. As you can imagine, the batter has hit the ball out in front of him. That's why the batter swings the bat barrel around with high speed. Do not let the ball get behind you. (Step #4) Now, he has finished hitting the ball with a wrist snap for the follow-through. His rear foot has turned around so he is on the toe of the rear foot.

194. *What about the finish up?*

For the last of the swing, the batter can now ease up on the front leg, but still try to keep the rear leg with no bend in it. Now, the follow-through, and it's on the way with lots of power. The batter can drop the bat and run for first base. Also, remember to drop the bat. Do not throw it. People have been hurt from this standard of action. Please notice that the front leg is slightly bent at the knee. This will be the leg that will give the batter that take-off power to first base.

195. *When using this method, does the batter have to swing the bat very fast at first?*

No. When trying this method of hitting, the batter does not have to swing the bat very hard at first because a hard swing is not important.

196. *Is a fast swing important in hitting the ball?*

Yes it is. When the pitcher is throwing the ball, he/she is supplying some of the power by the speed of the ball.

197. *Can you give me an example?*

Yes. An example of what I mean is to hold the bat in the hand and swing the bat no more than eight inches. When the ball hits the bat it will make a sharp snap sound. This is what the batter gets if he/she hits the ball at the right moment.

198. *What is the hardest pitch for a young person to hit?*

A curve ball.

199. *Why the curve ball?*

The curve ball can really scare a young person. Some swing at the curve ball when it is way outside the plate; others move away from the plate because of the fear of being hit by the ball. And most of the persons I talked with about the curve ball do not understand the curve, and ignorance of the curve ball can scare anybody.

200. *What is the hidden solution to hitting a curve ball?*

The secret is controlling the hands and holding back on the bat.

201. *What else should the batter know about the curve ball?*

Do not get impatient to hit the ball. Follow the curve ball all the way with the eyes and try not to swing at the ball if it is not going over the plate.

202. *How can I practice on the curve ball?*

After you have mastered using the Tee Master/Bat Master, get a friend who knows how to throw curve balls. Let him/her pitch curve balls to you. This is the main way to learn how to hit a curve ball. In my method of hitting, if you have learned all the techniques taught you—keeping your eyes on the ball and not getting scared—you will have control over the curve ball.

203. *What's the main thing the batter should think about on the curve ball?*

The main thing the batter should think about is holding the bat back. Then, as the ball approaches and the batter thinks it is close enough to reach, swing the bat.

204. *What if the curve ball is going outside? (Right-handed pitcher and right handed batter.)*

Do not swing the bat if the curve ball is going outside. Keep the bat held back.

205. *What if the ball is headed for my body? (Right-handed pitcher and right-handed batter.)*

> If it is headed for your body, stay in there and wait. Wait a second until you can't decide if it is going to curve or not. With time and a little experience, you will be able to tell if it will curve toward the outside corner or not. But stay in there, and do not be scared of getting hit by the ball. Keep your fear under control, for you have to do this if you want to hit the curve ball over the fence.

206. *Tell me of another way to practice with the curve ball.*

> Stand at the plate. You will not have a bat with you. Place your hands above your hips. Tell the pitcher to throw curve balls. While you are at the plate, you will stride and look at the ball. After a couple of days, or whenever you think you are ready, you can pick up the baseball bat.

207. *What is the reason for the batter not using a baseball bat?*

> The idea is to train the batter's eyes to follow the curve ball, and not to think about hitting the ball. When the eyes follow the ball automatically, go pick up the baseball bat. Once the eyes have gotten in the habit of following the ball, the batter should not be afraid to hit the ball. This is an excellent way to practice hitting the curve ball.

208. *Is flicking the wrist very important in the swinging of the baseball bat?*

> We don't think so. Bat speed is what we want. The front arm being bent and the rear arm with its force creates the accelerated bat speed we need. Have you ever tried flicking your wrist? It seems like it is practically inconceivable. You have just inches to move the wrist and that is not quite enough to create any sort of a flick motion with any amount of power.

209. *What if we called it "rolling the wrist" instead?*

> Rolling the wrist comes only after hitting the ball, wherever that may be. As far as we're concerned, that would be at the time of impact. The ball stays on the bat for only a split second, which would not help you that much anyway.

210. *Is there anything wrong with rolling the wrist?*

> Yes. The main thing we see wrong with this "wrist roll" idea is that the batter could roll the wrist just a little too early.

211. What is wrong with rolling the wrist too early?

The batter would be throwing the hit zone of the bat in the incorrect line of the swing. Never use the wrist roll, and the batter can hit the ball a whopping distance for a home run.

212. Tell us how to use the Tee Master/Bat Master?

We are going to use the Tee Master/Bat Master on the various pitches down the middle, outside, and inside pitches. Place the Tee Master on the outside corner of the plate (waist high). Take your proper plate coverage that you were taught in preceding pages. Now that you are a proper distance from the plate, place the "Hit Area" of the bat on the ball. You have taken your stance and stretched your arms at full length. You have not strided, and this has put you in line with the plate. The bat has hit the ball, and the rear hip is rotating and giving you more power in your hit.

213. Can you tell me exactly which curve ball is hardest to hit?

We have noticed that for a right-handed pitcher throwing to a right-handed batter, the curve ball outside is a tough one to hit.

QUESTION # 212, # 224

214. Why is the outside curve ball so important?

If the batter is a right-handed batter, this outside pitch is most important because it works perfect for the hit-and-run play. That's why most coaches want it hit. I will give an example. There is a runner on first base and only one out. This is where the coach has to decide on what to do. The coach takes a big chance if he/she lets the batter try for a home run, because the batter could hit the ball into a double play. The coach cannot risk having the batter bunt and throw away another out just to put a runner on second base, for then the next batter must get a base hit for the runner to score. So, the only thing left for the manager to do is to use the hit-run-play.

215. *So the manager gives the signal for the hit-and-run play, then what?*

This is what we do. With a runner on first base and as soon as the ball is let go by the pitcher, the batter attempts to hit the ball near second base or right field. Even if the batter misses the ball, the catcher will have a little more difficulty trying to throw the runner out going to second base.

216. *Why does the batter want to hit toward second base?*

With a right-handed batter at the plate and a base runner on first base, the second base player has to watch second base to catch the throw from the catcher.

217. *What about the shortstop playing second base?*

The shortstop cannot move because most right-handed batters hit between second and third base or into left field. Also, with a right-handed batter, the second base player has a habit of moving toward second if he/she sees the base runner on first about to run for second. Therefore, the second base player runs for second base to beat the base runner, having moved out of position too early. Now, with the second base player moving too early out of position, this leaves a tremendous opening between second and first base.

218. *What about the first base player?*

Well, the first base player has to stay close to first, because the base runner has to be watched so he/she cannot take a large lead off the base to get that extra jump to second base.

219. *What about this large opening between first and second base?*

    Now, this great opening between first and second base is where the batter wants to hit, and the only pitch that can go well to the opposite field is the outside ball. This is what we call "get ready for the hit-and-run play."

220. *Is the hit-and-run play that important?*

    Most definitely yes. Even before they start making the play, the batter will notice the second base player moving close to second base to catch the throw made by the catcher. The defensive team attempts to guess what the hit-and-run signal is form the coach. Even the pitcher throws the ball way outside so the batter can't hit the ball. And if the defensive team has picked up the signal and the ball is thrown way outside, the base runner will be thrown out and the ball will not be hit. Therefore, the coach makes sure the defensive team will not catch the signal.

221. *What else can happen on the hit-and-run play?*

    Well, if a hit is made, the runner on first goes to third and the batter reaches first base safely (runners at first and third). Now, we have a whole new baseball game with only one out.

222. *When using the Tee Master/Bat Master, how should the batter swing the bat on down-the-middle pitched balls? (Refer to picture)*

    On down-the-middle pitched balls, the swing of the bat will come from the shoulders, while the bat will go downward just a little bit. On this swing, the batter will keep the low pitches on the ground or on a low parallel line.

223. *On a pitched ball down-the-middle of the plate, what is the distance in front of the plate that the batter will hit this ball?*

    Go up to the plate and set your stance and stride. Move the bat out in front of the hands in the direction of the pitcher's mound. Now, the ball down-the-middle, as in the case of this model, is about thirteen inches in front of the plate. Look at the picture #222.

224. *When using the Tee Master/Bat Master where should the outside (waist high) ball be hit?*

QUESTION # 222, 223

The outside (waist high) ball should go in the direction of second base. When first starting out, the batter will probably hit to the left of the pitcher's mound. But in time, when the batter learns to improve his/her hand movements, the batter will end up hitting toward second base.

225. *What if the batter delays in hitting the ball with the bat? In what direction will the ball travel? (Right handed batter.)*

We want to draw attention to this: The longer the batter can delay in hitting the ball, and the more of the "Hit Area" of the bat that is angled toward right field (opposite field), the more the ball will travel down the right field line. Some of the top batters will do this on purpose, holding back on the swing of the ball, and hit the pitched ball down the first base line.

226. *Is this difficult to do?*

Yes. This is not as easy as it sounds or reads, but if the batter practices a lot, he/she will be able to do it.

227. *In what direction will the middle plate ball go when properly hit?*

In the case of a right-handed batter, the pitched ball will go in the direction of the shortstop. Not right at the shortstop, but in a line drive over the shortstop, just behind him/her to left center field. Some have a tendency of hitting this ball down the third base line. Watch yourself. Do not get in the habit of doing this. Habits are hard to break if not caught soon enough. Swing the bat as if going for the home run.

228. Should the batter try to place hit the ball?

No. Do not try to place hit the ball. Swing the bat wherever the ball is pitched, if in the strike zone. As for the direction of where the ball is going, get the "Hit Area" of the bat out there and it will take care of itself.

229. How many batters would you say know where they are hitting the ball?

A great percentage of batters just do not know where they should hit the middle pitched ball or the outside pitched ball. Of the players I asked, I could not find one player who knew where the inside pitched balls are hit. Whether they are the inside high or inside low, they just don't have any idea or don't care to know.

230. In what direction would the inside (waist high) pitched ball go if hit properly?

Take the position at the plate and go through the same procedure. Notice the model. The inside ball is about

QUESTION # 230 (Stance & Stride Device)

eighteen inches out in front of the home plate. Therefore, the ball should travel down the left field line or in the area of the third base player.

231. What should the batter be thinking about on the inside pitched ball?

Try and think of this: The "Hit Area" of the baseball bat is seven inches, not including the two inches from the top. As the "Hit Area" of the bat goes toward the ball to hit it and the closer it is inside the additional distance, the batter will have to go out in front of the home plate to hit the ball when pitched inside.

232. *Is there anything you can tell us about the arms being extended fully on the swing?*

Pertaining to the outside ball, the batter extends the arms fully. Now, on the ball down the middle-of-the-plate, the arms move in the direction of the pitcher. And on the inside ball, the batter will pull the arms in the direction of the third base player. (This will be opposite for left-handed batters).

233. *Is it possible to hit the inside ball close to the plate? (About seven inches).*

Yes. But on the inside ball, have the arms up against the body to hit the balls that are extremely close to the home plate. I have seen batters beat this inside ball, but they had to step in the direction of the third base line. As a result of this action, the stance opening is enlarged.

234. *What do you advise for hitting the inside pitch?*

If the batter steps the same distance every time, stepping forward in a straight line and doing this the same way all the time, the batter will hit the inside ball properly.

235. *What would the batter do if he/she wants to use the movable front foot?*

Stand about twenty-five inches away from the plate, which is nine inches farther away than our batter. The batter will take the step or stride in the direction of home plate on all balls pitched outside. Then step straightforward on all balls pitched down-the middle. On inside balls, the batter steps straightforward. Also, try to see how well it works, then use the techniques I have taught. Who knows? Maybe the batter can move that front foot back and forth in split-second speed. Good Luck! I can't tell you, so do as you please. The batter is the only one who can tell which technique is best for him/her.

236. *What do you want the batter to remember again about the step straightforward method?*

We want the batter to remember that outside pitched balls are not hit out in front of the plate the same as inside pitched balls. With different types of pitches, the batter has to start moving the hitting area of the baseball bat forward to hit the pitched ball. The player should understand these things before we can go any farther in this book.

237. *Can we review the critical aspects again of what we have just learned in the past question?*
Yes, but in a distinct procedure.

238. *Should the batter try to push the ball?*
No. Never try to push, overpower or force the ball.

239. *If the ball is pitched inside, where should it be going?*
Right-handed batters should hit the inside ball to left field. (Opposite field for left-handed batters.)

240. *If the ball is pitched outside, where should it be travailing?*
Right-handed batters should hit the ball to right field.

241. *Explain again about the rear hip or the hip closest to the catcher.*
For strength and accuracy, the hands should be in front of the rear hip.

242. *Should the hands be in front of the hips?*
Yes. As the baseball approaches, the batter starts swinging the bat and puts the hands forward as well as moving the front hip out of the way.

243. *Where should we hit the ball?*
Wherever the pitcher throws the ball (as long as it is a strike) is where the batter should hit the ball.

244. *How should we make our stride?*
Stepping straight forward toward the pitcher.

245. *How far should we step or stride?*
Seven inches and no more.

246. *If the batter wants to move the front foot or make it mobile, what should the batter keep in mind?*
If the hitter is right-handed batter, he/she should step straight forward on all pitched balls, except the outside ball; on outside balls, the batter should step in the direction of the plate or just a little toward first base.

247. *Is this very hard to do?*
We would say most definitely yes, because the batter will have to make a decision while the ball is in flight as to which way he/she wants to step. That does not give the batter much time to decide on which way to step.

248. *What happens if the batter guesses wrong?*

>The batter better practice how to fall down or get in the habit of getting out of the way very quickly. The batter might think to himself/herself that it is going to be an outside ball, but it turns out to be a screwball going for the face. KEEP IN MIND THAT THE BATTER CAN MOVE THE HANDS A LOT FASTER THAN THE FEET. Think about this, and we hope the batter gets the picture of what we mean about the movable front foot.

249. *How can batters trick themselves by using the Tee Master/Bat Master?*

>THIS IS THE MOST IMPORTANT QUESTION IN THE ENTIRE BASEBALL CHAPTER. BY TAKING MORE THAN ONE POSITION AT THE PLATE. DON'T MOVE YOURSELF IN A DIFFERENT POSITION AS THE BATTER MOVES THE TEE MASTER/BAT MASTER. WHEN THE BATTER IS AT THE PLATE, HE/SHE JUST DOESN'T HAVE THE TIME TO CHANGE POSITIONS ON EACH PITCH. SO WHY FOOL YOURSELF AND CHEAT? DO IT CORRECTLY, OR DON'T DO IT AT ALL.

250. *What makes the low outside ball so hard to hit (Picture No. 250)?*

>The batter will notice that the low outside ball is harder to hit because the batter has a tendency of not keeping his/ her eyes on the low outside ball. The batter will get lazy

QUESTION # 250

and not see the ball. THE BATTER MUST KEEP THE EYES ON ALL PITCHES AND MAKE SURE, ON THE LOW OUTSIDE PITCH, THAT THE "HIT AREA" OF THE BAT IS MOVING IN THE DIRECTION OF THE SECOND BASE PLAYER. DO NOT MAKE A SHORT SWING. THE IDEA IS TO FULLY EXTEND THE ARMS AND STRETCH OUT THERE FOR THE LOW OUTSIDE BALL, USING A THREE-QUARTER HORIZONTAL SWING.

251. Is the low inside pitch hard to hit (Picture No. 251)?

Yes, of course the low inside ball is hard to hit. But the batter has one thing in his/her favor if he/she hits it properly. The batter will get a greater distance for that home run ball on the inside low ball. Be sure that the stride is correct (seven inches) and that the batter gets the outside hip out of the way. AGAIN, HIT THE INSIDE BALL OUT IN FRONT OF THE PLATE. DON'T LET THE BALL PASS IN BACK OF YOU.

252. Is the outside hip very important on the low inside ball?

Yes. On all inside pitched balls, whether high, low or middle, the batter must get the outside hip out of the way. If the

QUESTION # 251 (Stance & Stride Device)

batter secures or holds the outside hip so it does not rotate out of the way, the batter cannot hit inside balls.

253. Where is the low inside ball supposed to go if hit properly?

Pertaining to a right-handed batter, the inside low ball should be blasted down third base.

254. How about the low ball down-the-middle?

If hit properly, the low ball in the middle should be hit in a line drive over shortstop or left center field.

255. *How about the outside low ball?*

> The outside low ball should go in the direction over second base if hit properly.

256. *What type of batter will the high pitched ball give trouble to in hitting?*

> A batter who over strides more than seven inches will have trouble with a high pitched ball. Also, the person who has any type of twitch will run into trouble.

257. *What is one of the arguments on trying to hit the high pitched ball?*

> One thought is that the hands should drop about five inches lower than what the model is doing, and the bat should be raised to the flight of the ball to get distance and height. (Picture No. 261)

258. *What's the other argument?*

> The other argument is that the hands should be held high, and the bat should be swung level with the flight of the ball.

259. *Which one do you think is better?*

> WE ARE 100% FOR HOLDING THE HANDS HIGH, SWINGING THE BAT LEVEL WITH THE FLIGHT OF THE BALL.

260. *What advice can you give the batter about holding the hands high with the flight of the ball (Horizontal Swing)?*

> Since the batter is just beginning, use the hands high and swing level with the ball. Then, when the batter gets more experience in hitting, he/she can attempt dropping the hands and raising the swing of the bat a little. Then the batter can decide for himself/herself which one is better for him/her to use, for we are all different. Remember, I am giving the batter the essential foundation for that home run ball and no strikeouts. It all depends on how much the batter practices (in the indicated technique) with my inventions, as to make him/her the best hitter in the league.

261. *Can the Tee Master/Bat Master help the batter on the high pitched ball?*

> Yes, if the batter does the same thing on the various high pitches. By placing the Tee Master/Bat Master on the inside

QUESTION # 261

corner, then in the middle, then on the outside corner of the plate, the batter will be in the same position to hit the ball as he/she is with the low ball area and the waist ball area.

262. *IS IT TRUE THEN, THAT THE DISTANCE THE BATTER PLACES THE BALL IN FRONT OF THE PLATE DOES NOT CHANGE ON THE VARIOUS TYPES OF PITCHES?*

YES, IT IS TRUE. WHETHER A HIGH, LOW OR MIDDLE PITCH, THE DISTANCE DOES NOT CHANGE.

263 *How long should the batter practice with the Tee Master/Bat Master per day?*

We would say not much more than twenty minutes per day. We suggest the batter use this as a guide. If the batter wants to practice more, then go ahead, but keep on a schedule.

264. *How long should the batter practice swinging a bat?*

Take another twenty minutes for swinging the bat. Do this in front of a mirror, but make sure you stay a good distance from the mirror. We don't want any broken mirrors.

265. *How long should the batter practice striding?*

Practice striding about twenty minutes, as well. Keep the hands just above the hips. Do not use a baseball bat for this exercise. Use the Stance and Stride Device or Bat Master.

266. *Is it good to practice with a friend?*

Yes. When you practice with a friend, you will be able to see each other's mistakes that need to be corrected.

267. *Can my mother or father help?*

Yes. Your mother or father should read this book so that they will be able to help you. I tried making this book easy to read for everybody, so we hope, if they enjoy baseball as much as I do, they will enjoy reading this book and will be able to be of great help to you.

268. *What should the coach tell the players about their shoulders on high pitched balls?*

Tell the players not to drop their shoulders on the high pitched balls, but to rotate the shoulders level with the height of the ball as they swing the bat.

269. *Is it true that the smaller the batter the closer he/she should stand to the plate?*

Yes. The smaller a baseball player is, the closer he/she should stand to the plate.

270. *Should the batter guess at what the pitcher is going to throw?*

No. Do as you have been taught in this book, and guessing will be something of the past. The batter will have plenty of time to hit the ball.

271. *Are the hands used for timing the pitched ball upon impact?*

Yes, the hands are what the batter uses for timing the swing.

272. *If the hands are used for timing upon impact, what is the stride used for?*

The stride is used as a gauge for the speed of the ball. If thrown slow, stride slow.

273. *Should the batter be making any movements at the plate when the pitcher winds up?*

Keep yourself still at the plate, with no movement of the bat. The shoulders, hands and all other parts of the body should be held still when the pitcher starts his/her wind up.

274. *When should the batter start gripping the baseball bat tightly when getting ready to swing the bat?*

The batter should raise the bat off the shoulder and grip it tightly when the pitcher is in the wind-up ready to pitch the ball.

275. *What pitch should the batter be ready for at all times?*

Be ready for the curve ball and the batter will not be caught off guard.

276. *Up to what point should the batter keep the eyes on the ball?*

Keep the eyes on the ball at all times. As the expression goes, "Even to see it come of the baseball bat upon impact."

277. *Should the batter glance back at the catcher to see if he/she can see the signals?*

No, because if the batter happens to guess wrong, such as if the batter thinks it is going to be an outside curve and the pitcher throws a fast ball inside, the batter might be in trouble. Always keep the eyes on the ball, not on the catcher's signals.

278. *When bunting the ball, what should the batter remember?*

When bunting, do not forget hand control, stride and stance. Do not pick up bad habits and get lazy. Bunting is only five percent of hitting; the balance should be used for hitting the ball with a full power swing. Bunting will be discussed later in the book.

279. *Should the batter try to place hit the ball?*

No. Swing the bat where the ball is going to be pitched. Do not try to place hit the ball.

280. *With runners on base, should the batter try for a base hit?*

When there are runners on base, try to hit the ball if the count is in the batter's favor. Here is an example: If the batter has two balls and one strike, or no strikes and one ball, take a good swing at the ball or hit for a home run, but make sure it is all right with the coach by first checking the signals.

281. *Should the batter swing on the third strike?*

Yes. Do not let the third strike go by. Swing at the third strike whether it is a couple of inches inside or outside, because umpires get selective on the third strike if the batter does not swing.

282. *What should the coach be watching for in the batter?*

Watch the hips and tell the batters if they are getting the full power out of the hip action.

283. *What else should the coach be looking for?*

Look for over striding. The team average will climb if the coach can make the batter's stride no more than seven inches.

284. *Is the batter's head important to the coach?*

Yes. If the batter is not careful it will destroy the complete swing. The head is the strong point of the batter. A batter should not take his/her eyes off the ball at any time. Watch the batter's head and make sure the head is facing in the direction of the pitcher when the swing is completed. If the head is in the direction of the pitcher when the swing is completed, that shows that the batter's eyes are on the ball.

285. *Should the coach use the hit-and-run play a lot?*

We would. But try not to be scared when using the hit-and-run play. If the coach uses the play, the players will hit 20% better than if the coach let them try to pick the various pitches to hit for themselves.

286. *After becoming "expert" on the Tee Master/Bat Master, what should the batter practice next?*

Try to find a pitcher who has good pitching control and have balls pitched to the batter. This will build up confidence in the batter. Have the balls pitched at average speed at first; then ask the pitcher to pitch the ball a little faster each time. Now, if the batter cannot find someone to pitch to him/her, then the batter can go to those places that have pitching machines. The machines only pitch down-the-middle balls, so the batter will not be able to practice on the curve ball.

287. *What proof do you have that this method of hitting is best?*

The most important thing is the Bat Master. We have tried other methods, but, in our opinion, this is the best technique ever used if the batter is going to use any type of baseball batting tee. In using the Baseball Batting Tees or Bat Master, here are some various methods the batter can experiment with when hitting. Mainly, the stride and the stance should be the first concern. Some have said, "What works for one player may not work for another." This doubtful, undemonstrated, unresolved statement might be accepted as a diminutive remark. I have analyzed various methods from the beginning to the end and this is the best, far-reaching method. I will discuss the various other methods with you. In this experiment the batter can use only the Tee Master. The Bat Master was designed for only one type of stance and stride (straightforward).

BEFORE STARTING, READ QUESTION #249 AGAIN.

288. What about the stance?

> The only stance we have talked about is the box or the step-straightforward stance. There are also two other basic stances—the narrow/closed and the wide/open stance.

289. What about the open/wide stance?

> With the model on this page, I have set the stance at twenty-five inches, similar to our box stance. I want the batter to look at the model's right foot. His position is much closer to the plate than in my method. The reason is because he will have to reach outside pitches with this stance. It will force the batter to hit to only one field. In this case, he will hit to left field only.

290. Is the wide/open stance good for pitches down-the middle and inside balls?

> Yes. As you place the Tee Master in various parts of the plate, the batter will notice that this type of stance is well

QUESTION # 289 (WRONG)　QUESTION # 291 (WRONG)

> suited for pitches that are in the middle and for inside balls.

291. What about the outside ball and the wide/open stance (Picture #292)?

> When it comes to outside balls, the wide/open stance is very clumsy. The wide/open stance is used by a lot of ball players because of their failure to hit outside pitches. When a batter uses this stance, it is like he/she is saying, "There will be no doubt in my mind that I can hit the inside and

middle pitched balls, but with the outside ball, I'll do my
best to hit that type of pitch." The stance is not good
because they will step down the third base line too often.

292. *Explain about the wide or open stance and the outside corner*
pitch.

On the outside corner pitch, the batter will notice that he/
she will have to get in the habit of "leaning" in the direction

QUESTION # 292 (WRONG)   QUESTION # 296 (WRONG)

of the outside pitch in order to hit the ball with any amount
of power.

293. *What about the wide or open stance and the ball being pitched*
outside. Will it go to the opposite field?

Now, using the wide or open stance, it will be more difficult
for the batter to hit the outside ball to the opposite field.
This is due to the angle of the bat when it comes in contact
with the ball.

294. *What about the narrow or close stance batter (Picture #296)?*

On this stance, the front foot is place nearer to the plate
than the back foot. This is based upon the fact that the
batter strides the front foot in the direction of the plate.
With this type of stance, the batter will have to stand a
greater distance away from the plate.

295. *What happens if the batter gets closer to the plate using the*
narrow or closed stance?

When the batter gets closer to the plate, he/she will not
be able to hit the inside pitched ball, because the front hip
is in a locked position.

296. *What is it that you don't like about the closed/narrow stance?*
If you notice the model on the previous page, he has the closed/narrow stance. He cannot reach the outside ball on the Tee Master unless he steps or strides toward the plate. Stepping in the direction of the plate worried us, because we noticed that the batter got in the habit of stepping in the direction of the plate all the time. In doing that, he could not get the outside or front hip out of the way correctly, which therefore prevented him from hitting the inside ball.

297. *What do you like about the narrow/closed stance?*
That the batter can (wee) hold back on the bat longer, keeping it out of the hitting area. On the wide/opened stance or box stance, the batter cannot do this as proficiently.

298. *What about the outside pitched ball?*
On the outside balls, the narrow/closed stance is a (wee) better idea than the wide/opened stance or box stance.

299. *On the inside pitch balls, which stance is better?*
On the inside pitch balls, the wide/opened stance is (wee) preferred over the narrow/closed or box stance.

300. *Which stance should the batter choose as the ideal stance?*
WE HIGHLY RECOMMEND THE BOX OR STEP-STRAIGHTFORWARD CONCEPT, BECAUSE (I SAY IT AGAIN) THE BATTER DOES NOT HAVE THE TIME TO CHANGE HIS/HER STANCE FOR EACH PITCHED BALL. Remember, when picking one of the three stances, the batter will have to pick one and stay with it. But do as I have instructed the batter to get the maximum extent of use out of each stance. There is not a single pitch (high, low, or middle) that we can think of that will handicap the step-straight-forward method, as opposed to the open/wide stance or the closed/narrow stance. LET'S REDUCE OR ELIMINATE THE STRIKEOUT AND SELECT THE STEP-STRAIGHT-FORWARD STYLE IN HITTING.

301. *Can you tell us more about the stride and stance?*
The stride must be finished before the outside hip starts rotating and before the bat enters the hitting area. Also, at the end of the stride the shoulders start turning.

302. *Are the stride and stance very important to the swinging of the bat?*

> YES. WE ARE CONVINCED THAT THE STRIDE AND STANCE ARE VERY SIGNIFICANT FOR THE SWING; IN FACT, THEY ARE SO SIGNIFICANT THAT THEY ARE THE ESSENCE OF THE BATTER'S HITTING.

303. *Is it true that if the batter's feet are wrong the batter can't hit the ball properly?*

> YES. IF THESE THINGS DO NOT WORK TOGETHER IN UNISON (THE STRIDE, STANCE AND HANDS), THE ENTIRE SWING WILL BE WRONG. THAT IS WHY THEY SAY, "IF THE BATTER'S FEET OR STANCE ARE INCORRECT, THE BATTER CAN'T HIT THE BALL PROPERLY." IN CONCLUSION, WE SAY, "THERE IS NO LIMIT TO WHAT THE PLAYER CAN ACCOMPLISH IN BASEBALL. PRACTICE WHAT I HAVE TAUGHT THE BATTER—SO HE/SHE CAN BECOME THAT CHAMPION IN BASEBALL HITTING.

HOW TO MASTER BUNTING

304. What is the definition of bunting the ball?
Without swinging the bat, the batter hits the ball very lightly into the infield.

305. Is bunting important in the baseball game?
Most definitely, yes.

306. How many different types of bunts are there?
Two types mainly. The sacrifice bunt and the drag-type bunt.

307. What is the sacrifice bunt?
When the hitter stands at the plate with both feet flat on the ground, or flat-footed, the batter will try to bunt the ball, not caring if he/she is put out, but only trying to advance the runner on base, mainly a runner on first base. That is why it's called a sacrifice bunt. The batter puts himself/herself out in order to advance the runner.

308. Would this affect the batting average of the batter?
No. In this sort of a situation, the batter will not be charged "with a time at bat," meaning that if the batter is put out, it will not go against the batting average. It would be considered as if the batter never had gone to bat.

309. What about the drag-bunt?
This is when the hitter attempts to run as the ball is bunted. The batter is not making a sacrifice, because no runners are advancing or the coach did not give the batter the signal to bunt the ball for a sacrifice. If the batter happens to run out the drag-bunt and makes it to first base and no infielder made a mistake on the play, the batter is given credit with a base hit.

310. What happens if the batter is put out?

> If the batter happens to be put out, some scorekeepers will count it as a sacrifice hit and will not count it as a "time at bat."

311. Is that very fair?

> We feel that any drag-bunt is an attempt to get a hit, and if the batter is put out it should be scored as a "time at bat."

312. Will the defensive team be ready for a bunt if a runner is on first base with no outs?

> Yes. The defensive team will be ready for a bunt because it is the expected thing to do in this type of situation.

313. How can the batter avoid letting the defensive team know that he/she is not going to bunt the ball?

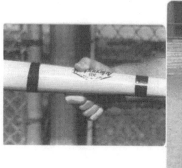

QUESTION # 316   *QUESTION # 313, 320*

> Following the pitcher's wind up and right after the ball is released and it is in flight, at that moment the batter will move the body into the bunt position.

314. How would the batter hold the baseball bat?

> In a horizontal position.

315. How is the bat held with the left hand for a right-handed batter?

> The bat is held in a sort of relaxed type grip, but firmly.

316. How does the batter hold the bat with the right hand (right-handed batter)?

> Holding the bat with the thumb and index finger only, the batter will gather back the other three fingers into the palm of the right hand (like holding a toy pistol) so with the very end of the thumb, and bending the index finger, the batter will hold the bat. This will form sort of a "V."

317. Why is the "V" so important?

So that when the ball hits the bat, the impact will slide the bat into the "V" or crevice of the thumb and index finger.

318. What will that do to the speed of the ball?

This will reduce the speed of the ball. This reduced speed will let the batter put the bunt a few feet from the plate and the catcher will have a hard time getting to the ball in a hurry. Also, it will be a good distance from the third base player, pitcher or first base player. It also makes it hard for the players to grab the ball and throw it to second base in order to destroy the sacrifice bunt.

319. What mistake do most batters make when trying to bunt the high pitched ball?

A great number of ball players get low, in the squatted position, to bunt with the bat held below the "torso" or "chest." Now, if a high pitch is thrown, with the batter being in this squatted position, the batter will not have time enough to lift the bat up above the ball, then dropping it down again. This is why the ball goes into the air. The batter is forcing the bat up because of being in the squatted position. This is the natural thing to do, but the batter will make a very poor bunter.

320. How should the batter bunt the high pitched ball?

The bat should be even with the shoulders, while the batter is standing up as straight as possible. With the bat being this high above the strike area, the batter should push the ball towards the ground with the bat. When bunting, there is no problem at all in bending the knees to bring down the bat to meet the ball with a horizontal stroke.

321. Why don't they bunt more in the big league games?

Bunting is something of the past in big league baseball because they have the "special inning," which is going to win the ball game for them. When I see all the mistakes they make in hitting, I can understand this idea. In little league and high school baseball, the coach can't depend on the "special inning." Therefore, the bunting game is most important.

322. How does the batter bunt down the first base line?

Note the illustration. The right-handed batter just pulls the right arm next to the body, positions the bat toward the first base line, then controlling the bunt of the ball down toward first base.

QUESTION # 322   *QUESTION # 323*

323. *How does the batter bunt down the third base line?*

    The right-handed batter pulls the left arm close to the body, positions the bat toward third base then controlling the bunt of the ball in that direction.

324. *Does a person have to know the basics of bunting before they can be taught to bunt in different directions?*

    Yes. The most significant thing in bunting is putting the bat on the ball, stopping the high speed of the ball, and letting the ball fall almost dead. To do this, the batter has to pull the bat close to the body at the time of impact with the ball.

325. *Can the coach use the bunt on the hit-and-run-play?*

    Yes. Take this example: We know that the defensive team is waiting for a bunt. The catcher, pitcher, first base player, and third base player will all get ready to lunge in for the bunt. Now, we have a runner on first base, with no outs. Since we know this, we give the signal to the base runner to run on the first, second or third pitch. It will all be decided when we think that the pitcher will not throw away the ball in order to catch our runner stealing. Various things will take place on the defensive team as our base runner starts moving toward second. The second base player, thinking that our runner is going to run, will get scared and run for second base; the first base player can't decide whether or not he/she should come into get the doubtful bunt, and the third base player will automatically come in anyway.

326. *Where does the batter bunt the ball if the first base player runs in for the bunt?*

> The third base line is where to bunt the ball. The third base player runs in and snaps up the ball, quickly looking at second base. The third base player sees the runner has made it safely, then he/she stares at first base. The third base player can't make the throw to first, for the first base player has rushed in and can't make it back to first in time to get the runner.

327. *What about the second base player?*

> Now, if the second base player did not make it to first in time, then there is no one to throw to. As the third base player is still wondering what to do, our runner has passed second and now has moved on to third, because the third base player is out of place and can't decide whom to throw to. This play can work many times if done properly. By moving the runner from first base to third base, the one bunting the ball is safe at first. On the next pitch, the runner on first runs for second.

328. *What is the "squeeze play"?*

> The defensive team now works what the ballplayers call the "squeeze play." With the two runners on base, the offensive team tries to make a score. When the offensive team ends up with a runner on third base and a runner on second base with only one out, the offensive team has the perfect chance to score two runs. By bunting the ball, the offensive team can drive the defensive team crazy.

329. *What should the offensive team do when they have a runner on first and a runner on second with no outs?*

> The offensive team will see the defensive team place the first base player in a closer position toward home, relying on the idea that the player can field the bunt. Then the offensive team pays attention to the third base player. With runners on first and second base and a bunt forthcoming, the third base player is not taught to stay close to third base. This is what they are taught: to not let the pitcher or first base player field the bunt and to make an attempt to force the play at third base. Also, by having the hitter pretend to bunt, this action will draw the third base player off the

base at least fifteen or twenty feet. When the offensive team has figured out how the third base player is going to move, then we give the signal to the batter to pretend to bunt. The coach gives a signal to the base runners at first and second to steal their next base. The ball is thrown by the pitcher. The base runner on first and second start running and the hitter moves into the bunt position. The third base player runs in toward home. When this player notices that it is a "fake bunt," the third base player attempts to run back to third base. Then the catcher normally makes a bad throw to the running third base player letting our runner who was running toward third score home.

330. *Does this type of play work in the big league baseball games?*

No. In the big leagues, players are taught how to cover for all plays with practically no errors. As for little league, high school or college, the offensive team can fool quite a few of the defensive teams with this plan. A lot of little league teams have no way of defending themselves against the bunting game. The players get very confused, bumping into each other, throwing the ball away. The defensive team can look very foolish against the bunting game.

331. *What type of baseball team would you like?*

With a team of good base runners plus good bunters, you can beat 85% of the teams in little league, even though my strong hitters are not too good. Now, if the team has read this baseball book, that could make the difference in the percentage, for they will know how to defend themselves from a bunting attack.

332. *What else can you tell us about bunting the ball?*

The batter will notice that with bunting, he/she can direct a ball by giving it an extra shove past the third base player who is running in, or the first base player. Also, a shove will hit the ball past the second base player who has left his/her position to get the throw at first base. Boys and girls really enjoy playing this type of baseball. The defensive team will make errors and get nervous if the team is bunting and running, and this will let the offensive team score a lot of runs.

HOW TO MASTER THROWING

333. Do all good throwers have something in common?
   Yes.

334. What is the first thing they have in common?
   The first thing they have in common is a proper stepping motion.

335. What about the forearm and wrist?
   Good throwers also have the ability to get a snapping motion out of the forearm and wrist with the fastest amount of speed.

336. What do the hips have to do with throwing the ball?
   The hips and foot come through on the throw as the player makes the finished throw.

337. What is the first thing the player should start working with in throwing?
   The feet.

338. What about the shoulders, hips and body?
   If the player gets in the habit of moving the front foot at an angle when throwing, the shoulders, hips, body and the rear leg will not come through correctly to support the arm.

339. What's wrong with stepping at an angle?
   If the player steps at an angle, it will shorten the throwing arm, making the player push on every throw. As a result, the arm will become sore. That is when the player strains the arm, probably requiring some time to heal and not being able to use it.

340. *Is it wrong to throw with another type of baseball other than the one you are going to play with in the baseball game?*

> Yes. Do not throw a baseball unless it is a standard type ball players are going to use in the baseball game, such as hard ball, soft ball, semi-hard ball, blooper ball, etc.

341. *Can the player throw the ball fast before warming up?*

> At first, do not throw the ball fast. Wait until the player has first thrown a few balls.

342. *Is it wrong to throw a tennis ball?*

> Yes. Do not use a light ball to throw with, such as a tennis ball or a golf ball.

343. *What happens if the throwing arm becomes tired or sore?*

> If a player damages the throwing arm in any way, he/she will probably not make the first team as a baseball player. So, please be careful with the throwing arm. Do not break any of the rules set forth in these instructions. These rules are very important.

344. *What of the picture called "Effective Throwing?"*

> With this type of throw, the player will be able to throw the ball with accuracy and a lot more speed. First, notice the way the model is gripping the ball. Now, notice the "forceful" area of the wrist and forearm. It is the forceful forward-type motion of the forearm and the wrist snap that will give the player extra speed for the effective throwing action without damage to the arm.

QUESTION # 344
EFFECTIVE THROWING

QUESTION # 345   QUESTION # 346

345. Explain how the player would throw the ball.

Look at the next three pictures. In the first picture, the model is in the throwing position with the ball brought back; his shoulders are turned; he has raised the ball just in back of his ear. Now, notice how his feet are positioned. The player raises the front foot only slightly off the ground as he/she strides.

346. What about the second picture called "Stepping Ahead"?

In this picture, the player is now stepping ahead, bringing around his hip, shoulders, rear leg and rear foot at the same time. The forearm is raised level with the shoulders.

347. What about the picture called "Release Point?"

In this picture, the model has now completed his throw, as the arm is at the point of follow through. The player is showing you about where the point is to release the ball. If this had been a real throw, this picture would have captured the release point of the baseball.

QUESTION # 347

348. Is it important to keep the elbow up level with the shoulder as in the picture "Stepping Ahead?"

Yes. Never let the elbow of the arm drop below the line of the shoulders in the action of throwing.

349. Why is this important?

Because if the elbow does fall below the shoulders the player will have shortened the arc of the throw, making the point of release come to soon. The ball will be thrown either very high or far off the target.

350. *Are the wrist and forearm that important in the throw?*

Yes. A lot of people just do not believe that the wrist and forearm give the player almost seventy percent of his/her throwing power. If the player coordinates the legs, shoulders and hips correctly, the player can add power, but they are only supplements to the act of throwing. They are essential factors, but the main factors are the wrist and forearm.

351. *What is the secret of adding speed to the ball when throwing?*

When the player advances the speed of the forearm and the wrist, the high speed of advancing is what gives the player the power of the throw. By increasing the forearm speed plus the wrist snap just before releasing the ball, the player has the secret he/she needs for that added power.

352. *What should the player do to take care of the arm?*

Wear a sweatshirt as much as possible. Do not let the arm cool off too fast. Put on a sweater or a warm-up jacket. If the player gets a sore arm, give it a rest.

353. *What shouldn't the player do to the arm if it is sore?*

Do not apply any form of heat, unless it is really serious. Do not have it rubbed down or *massaged.*

354. *Is there anything wrong with throwing sidearm?*

Yes. Throw overhand, using the three-quarter style. That way, the player can fit into any position on the team. Sidearm throwers are something of the past. Three-quarter style is of the future.

355. *What's wrong with throwing sidearm?*

The player will not make it as an outfielder. A sidearm thrower will not be able to throw the distance necessary to play outfield and will not have the accuracy. For third base and shortstop, the player will not have the necessary preciseness in his/her throw.

356. *What about being catcher?*

Have you ever seen a catcher that throws sidearm? Such a player would be throwing curve balls to the second base player.

357. *What position can the sidearm thrower play?*

The only positions the sidearm thrower will be able to play are second base and maybe first base.

358. What is the one way to practice throwing?

One of the ways to improve your forearm speed and wrist snap is to get a chair, mark off twenty feet (depending on age of the person), then sit down in the chair. Now, start throwing balls at the Super Strike Master or Super Strike Master Jr. using your forearm and wrist snap as much as possible with fast speed. Also, in place of the Super Strike Master, you might have a friend sit in a chair so you two can play catch. Instructions for the assembly of the Super Strike Master, Super Strike Master Jr. and Stepping Square are at the end of the chapter.

359. Does the player throw with his/her feet?

Yes. But let us explain: IF THE FEET ARE NOT PLACED PROPERLY, THE PLAYER CANNOT THROW PROPERLY. Also, the stance and stride in hitting is the same in throwing, except you pivot on the rear foot in hitting.

360. What is the "Stepping Square?"

It is a square that is adjustable up to 60 inches in length. This square is what will teach the player how to stride properly as he/she throws the ball. It is called PROPER FOOT MOVEMENT. The Stepping Square will make the

STEP # 1　　　　　　　　　　　　STEP # 2

STEP # 3　　　　　　　　　　　　STEP # 4

QUESTION # 360-363

player step straight ahead in the direction he/she is throwing, so he/she can hit the target with proper accuracy. The player can also use the Stepping Square in connection with the

Super Strike Master and Super Strike Master Jr., placing one inside the Bat Speed Apparatus or Backstop Master. Mark off twenty feet through sixty feet and start throwing at the target. Remember, practice, practice, to be a CHAMPION IN THE ART AND SCIENCE OF THROWING.

361. *What about the rear foot and the "Stepping Square?"*

Now, if the player wants to keep a smooth motion with the throw, the rear foot is pulled along the ground, for it assures that the body gets behind the throw of the ball. We think the "Stepping Square" is the best device we have for teaching throwing with the feet.

362. *What is it that people do wrong when throwing the ball?*

The greatest fault that most young players have is drifting the rear foot, instead of pulling it. Also, stepping at an angle, crossing the left foot—as it pertains to a right-handed player—in front of the right foot. The player is not able to throw unrestricted and loose because it ties him/her up on the follow through, or when finishing up on the throw.

363. *Will the "Stepping Square" improve my accuracy?*

Most definitely. Some good throwers have said that it has improved their accuracy by thirty-five percent.

HOW TO MASTER CATCHING

364. *How would the player catch a ball in the area between the waist and the top of the head?*

QUESTION # 364, 365   QUESTION # 366, 367

If the ball is hit in a straight line the player wants to extend the arms at full length and have the fingers of the glove straight at the ball. The palm of the glove is facing down. Now, just before the ball goes into the glove pull the glove back toward yourself in order to cushion the impact of the ball.

365. *What should the player do with the other hand, the one without the glove?*

The player should use it to trap the ball right after he/she catches it. Notice illustration.

366. *How would the player catch a ball below the waist area?*

Notice the picture. Catches in this area should have the fingers of the glove straight at the ball and the palm of the glove is facing up.

367. *How does the player use the hand without the glove?*

Just as the player did before, use the ungloved hand as a trap to keep the ball from bouncing out of the glove. The player does not want to use the ungloved hand too soon or else the ball will hit the fingers, so be careful.

368. *What will happen if the player puts the palm of the glove facing down when catching a ball below the waist?*

If he/she does this, the player cannot follow the ball into the glove. The player will lose sight of the ball temporarily before catching it. Then his/her judgment will be off and the player might drop the ball.

369. *What else should the player do before catching the ball?*

Just prior to catching the ball, keep the glove wide open. A lot of players are in the habit of putting the thumb of the glove close to the pocket and not fully opening up the glove.

370. *After doing everything right and the player still drops the ball, what could the player be doing wrong?*

Something very simple. The player is taking his/her eyes off the ball at the last second just before the ball is in the glove. Keep the eyes on the ball all the way into the baseball glove.

371. *How should the player place the feet when catching the ball?*

As in each picture, the player has his feet ready to throw the ball the moment it is caught. So, when catching a ball, try to have the feet properly placed in order to get rid of the ball the moment it is caught.

372. *What about the picture "The Bucket Catch?"*

If balls are hit high in the air they are called "pop-ups" or "flies." Sometimes foul balls are "pop-ups." In the picture, the player uses his glove like a "bucket" ready to catch the ball. The ball is falling in the direction of the glove. The player wants to pull down on the glove and move the

QUESTION # 372

elbows near the side of the body as the ball approaches. This is how the "bucket" is formed. The player should follow the ball all the way into the glove with the eyes and he/ she will never be caught dropping a fly or pop-up.

373. *On this type of catch, what do a lot of players do wrong?*
Some players have the tendency of putting the glove in front of their face to catch the ball at the last moment. This is dangerous because the player can temporarily lose sight of the ball.

HOW TO MASTER FIELDING

QUESTION # 374

QUESTION # 376   QUESTION # 379

374. *What about the figure on fielding?*

In the illustration, the fielder has his hands on his knees, his legs are bent slightly, his eyes are on the batter, and he can move in any direction.

375. *What is a good saying for catching ground balls?*

Here are two. First, "Try to catch the ball to one side of the body or the other." Second, "The fielder must try to catch the ball out in front of the body."

376. *What about the illustration number 376?*

In the next illustration, the fielder is catching the ball in front. The right foot is in the direction pointed straight ahead. He moves his left foot—or back foot—in a ninety-degree angle. In order for the fielder to catch the ball, he has to bend his knees.

377. Why should he bend his knees?

This will allow him to reach the ball.

378. Why is it called the "Take-in" method?

Because the player's legs are in a position where the ball cannot pass through the legs very easily. The player is stopping the ball almost completely. The player must also put the glove flat on the ground to make the catch complete, with the right hand on top of the glove so that when the ball enters the glove, it will be taken-in. This is for a player who throws right-handed.

379. What exercise would you recommend to practice to get in the habit of placing the glove flat on the ground?

Put the right hand behind the back and let someone hit the infielder ground balls. The fielder will then get in the habit of putting the glove flat on the ground. It is hard to do at first, but once the fielder gets the trick of it, he/she will be a better infielder. (Reverse if the fielder throws left-handed.)

380. What should the stance be or how far apart should the fielder spread the feet?

It will vary according to the size of the fielder and what makes him/her feel comfortable; but measure from the rear foot inside heel to the front foot; measure the back heel.

381. What about the next picture?

The fielder straightens the legs and raises the ball up. The next step is done all in one motion. As the fielder

QUESTION # 381   *QUESTION # 382*

straightens up, he draws the arm ready to throw. He then throws as he steps with the front foot.

382. *What of picture #382?*

The front foot has now stepped. Until the fielder makes the throw, the front foot will stay on the ground. Now, when the fielder throws the ball, raise the front foot only a few inches from the ground.

383. *Why should the fielder raise the front foot only a few inches?*

The front foot should not be raised high for this will cause a delay in the throwing and that we do not need.

384. *After the foot is raised, in what direction should it be pointed?*

When the fielder raises the front foot only a few inches, he/she should make sure that it is headed in the direction he/she is throwing. If it is not in line with the throw, the ball will go in the direction the foot is pointed, not in the direction of the throw. This is most important in throwing. READ THIS PARAGRAPH AGAIN IF YOU DO NOT UNDERSTAND, AND STUDY THE PICTURES.

385. *How about getting ground balls in the infield?*

If the infielder can, in any way possible, get in front of the ball while it is hit on the ground or hit in the air for a pop-up.

386. *Can you give me an example?*

Yes. Now, let's say the player is the shortstop. The ball is hit hard on the ground directly to the left, or near second base. Make a quick angle and cut the ball off in order to place yourself ahead of the ball.

387. *What should the player remember when playing infield?*

Squat down low when playing the ground ball.

388. *Why should the infielder squat down low?*

Remember that once the infielder is low, it is a lot easier to come up on the ball. That is, if the ball should take a bad bounce like hitting a rock, or if the ball should take a high bounce, the infielder has an easy chance to come up on the ball to catch it.

389. *Should the infielder always be ready for the ball to take a bad bounce?*

No. Don't think every ball will jump. It just doesn't work that way. Play the ball for a grounder, not expecting it to jump. But, if it does, the infielder should be ready in plenty of time to catch it.

390. *Should the infielder take the front foot off the ground when throwing the ball?*

No. Try not to take the front foot off the ground until the infielder is just about ready to throw the ball. This is because the infielder has to step and throw at about the same time.

391. *What should I do if I don't have much time to throw the ball?*

Bring yourself upright when you are getting ready to throw the ball. But, if you happen to be in a hurry, you can throw the ball underhand if you are close enough to the base where you are throwing.

392. *What things should the infielder think about when fielding the ball?*

When fielding the ball, be careful, but hurry. Take a tight grip on the ball and throw as precisely as possible.

393. *If the ball is hit hard, will the infielder have time to catch the runner?*

If the ball is hit fairly hard, the infielder will have sufficient time to catch and throw the ball before the runner can make it to first base.

394. *What if the ball is hit slowly?*

If the ball is hit slowly, then the infielder will have to move fast to catch the runner. Do not think you always have a lot of time to throw. The infielder should have to hurry for all hits, fast or slow, thinking to himself/herself, "That player is the fastest runner I have ever seen." Be accurate and careful in all your infielding.

395. *Is there another type of method used in the infield to catch ground balls?*

Yes. The "Flow Step." It has a ten-inch wider step than the "Take in" method.

QUESTION # 395

396. *What have you discovered about the "Flow Step" method?*

The "Flow Step" has a wider stance. It is excellent for youngsters over fourteen years of age.

397. *Why is the "Flow Step" good for youngsters over fourteen years of age?*

Because by the time youngsters are fourteen years of age, they should have the strength to throw off their rear leg. Not all youngsters are the same. Some take longer to develop strength. Now, try them both and see which one of the methods you like.

398. *What happens if the infielder widens the stance on the "Take-in" method?*

If the infielder opens up the stance seven inches, it will give the infielder a better stance to bend down ahead of the ball when it is hit by the batter.

399. *What sort of practice should I use to get me in the habit of keeping low when infielding?*

Bend down as low as you can with your buttocks close to the ground and start walking around. The lower you can get the better. If you are down low, it is a lot easier to come up if the ball should jump by hitting a rock. Do the exercise that we just described. Open up the "Take-in" stance seven or nine inches and keep your eyes on the ball. As you progress on this exercise, put your hands behind your back.

400. *What else should the infielder remember that you feel will help him/her?*

Remember, the infielder has to get his/her hands out in front. Teach yourself to pull the ball toward you after catching the ball; then you will have the answer to becoming an excellent infielder.

401. *What other way can I practice to become a good infielder?*

One way is to have a friend hit ground balls to you from one side to the other, making you move in all directions to aid you in becoming an excellent infielder. You must practice, practice. Also, follow that ball all the way with your eyes into your baseball glove.

HOW TO MASTER PITCHING

402. *What should I have to think about to be a successful pitcher?*
    In being a successful pitcher, a player should think about how he/she can out-guess the hitter when throwing the ball.

403. *How does the pitcher out-guess the hitter?*
    The pitcher should try to pitch the ball where the batter does not think it will be pitched. By this, we mean throwing a change-up pitch when a fastball is expected, or a fastball when a sinker pitch is expected. Using this idea is call "mixing up the pitches."

404. *Do many pitchers use this method?*
    Yes. Many pitchers use this method, always trying to throw pitches to the batter's weakest area of hitting.

405. *How does the pitcher know a batter's weakest area of hitting?*
    The weak areas are figured out by trial and error. For example, a batter will hit the ball off the home run wall. As the pitcher comes in after the inning, the coach will say to the pitcher and catcher, "What did you throw to that batter?" The pitcher might say, "It was a fastball, waist-high, inside." The coach will groan and say, "Never again! Don't ever let that batter have that type of pitch." Then the manager will get out a notebook and write down (Name) hits fastballs, waist-high inside. After a few notations of this type, the manager will have all of the batters noted as to what to pitch or what not to pitch to each of them. Then, before each game, the manager will take out the list of the team

members they are playing for the day, and go over each batter separately to tell the pitcher where to throw each pitch for each batter. Then the fielders are told, "(Name) will hit to left field on the low-outside fast ball," etc. This idea of trial and error does not always work, but at least it is helpful.

406. *Being a fielder, does this help me at all?*

Yes, the fielders know where to place themselves so that when a batter comes up to hit, the signals will be relayed by the catcher and the pitcher. Now, if the fielders know where the pitcher is going to throw the ball, the infielders and outfielders will place themselves in the proper position for that batter. The reason is because they can then guess just about where the batter is going to hit the ball.

407. *What can the batter do to defend himself/herself?*

Well, in big league baseball, the batter changes plate position (from a left-handed batter to a right-handed batter). That is known as a "switch hitter." Use the Tee Master/Bat Master for practicing to be a switch hitter.

408. *If, being the coach, I don't have the time to make a note of each batter, what can I do?*

In subsequent questions, the coach will get some advice on what to pitch to each batter as they come to the plate.

409. *What is the first question the pitcher should ask himself/herself as the batter comes up to the plate?*

Take note of the batter to see if that person has full plate coverage.

410. *What if the batter stands too far from the plate?*

Pitch outside to the batter if the batter is standing too far from the plate. The pitcher will not need the curve ball. Throw the batter a fastball outside. The batter can't hit it if it can't be reached.

411. *What is the second thing the pitcher should look for in the batter?*

Look to see if the batter is over striding—that is, moving the front foot more than seven inches. Also, while over striding, notice if the batter bends forward and dips the front shoulder.

412. *What if the batter does over stride, bend forward, and dips the shoulders?*

> In that case, give the batter a high and inside pitch and even a decent foul ball won't be hit.

413. *Why can't the batter hit the high and inside pitch?*

> The reason is that the batter cannot move the bat fast enough to get out in front of the ball. So keep the fastball in close and high on the batter who over strides.

414. *What if the pitcher gives the batter a low pitch?*

> A batter who over strides can hit low balls better than a batter who does not over stride. DO NOT PITCH A LOW PITCH TO A BATTER WHO OVER STRIDES.

415. *How can a batter who over strides hit a low pitch better?*

> Because the batter can hold the bat longer in the lowball area of the strike zone.

416. *How about a change-of-pace pitch to a batter who over strides?*

> The pitcher can also throw a change-of-pace, or slow pitch, to a person who over strides by keeping it high and inside. This will throw the batter off balance and hurt his/her timing. Also, for a batter who is a very fast strider, the change-of-pace will handicap his/her hitting.

417. *What if the batter stands far from the plate and strides toward home plate or first base every time (right-handed batter)?*

> Pitch that batter the inside ball and the pitcher will not have much to worry about.

418. *What if the batter steps forward toward third base and is far from the plate (refer to pictures #289 and #291)?*

> Most of the time that batter cannot hit outside pitches.

419. *What if the batter is standing close to the plate and the legs are kept close together (closed stance). What type of pitch is thrown?*

> Pitch the ball inside at about the waist zone or belt area.

420. *What else can you teach the pitcher about the batter?*

> When the pitcher has mastered seeing the faults in stance and striding, then he/she is ready to look at hand movements and hip movements. When a batter is real nervous, there is a tendency to move. These movements are called "twitches."

421. *When are these "twitches" noticed most?*

>The time they are the most noticed is when the ball is about twenty feet or less away from home plate.

422. *Being the batter, what can these "twitches" do to my hitting?*

>They can negatively affect the batter timing when swinging the bat.

423. *Just what is a "hand twitch" exactly?*

>It is a hand movement. When the ball is in flight, the batter's hands will lower as the ball approaches.

424. *What type of pitch should the pitcher give this batter who has a "hand twitch?"*

>With this type of batter, pitch the ball high and inside. If the pitcher throws to that one spot all day, the bat will not get on the ball nor can anything be done about it.

425. *What if the batter "wiggles" or moves the bat back and forth. What type of pitch is given then?*

>If the batter waves the bat, moving it back and forth, or if the batter tilts the bat in any way, it will show that the bat is positioned improperly. If the batter gives any of these indications, throw the inside high pitch. Few pitchers take advantage of this type of mechanical weakness, so many batters have this hand movement or "twitch" every time they go to bat.

426. *What about a "shoulder twitch?"*

>This is a quick shoulder movement in the direction of the catcher when the ball is about twenty feet or less from the batter. This is the same type of mistake as made in the "hand twitch."

427. *What type of pitch does a batter get if there is a "shoulder twitch?"*

>All the pitcher has to do is pitch high inside fastballs and the batter cannot even touch the ball.

428. *What about a "leg twitch?"*

>When there is a "leg twitch," or movement of the leg, the pitcher will then pitch the high-inside fastball.

429. *What type of pitch does the batter get if there is a "hip twitch?"*

>When there is a "hip twitch," or movement of the hip, the pitcher will pitch the high-inside fastball as well.

430. *What if the batter with a "twitch" hits the high-inside fastball for a home run anyway?*

> Then it is the pitcher's misjudgment. Watch to make sure that the movement does not happen just as the pitcher is getting ready to release the ball or on the wind-up.

431. *I don't understand. Please explain?*

> Having this mechanical fault, the various types of "twitches" must take place while the ball is in flight or about twenty feet or less before the ball is to the batter. Now, if the "twitch" happens prior to that time, they will not be considered "twitches" and cannot be called mechanical faults. For example, if the batter is waiving the bat and then stops moving the bat prior to the twenty feet, it is not a "twitch." Therefore, the pitcher does not pitch that batter the high-inside fastball.

432. *Should the pitcher let someone change his/her pitching style?*

> If the fundamental pitching movements are correct, then they should not be changed. However, if the pitching movements are not correct, then the pitcher should have them changed.

433. *What about the arms in pitching?*

> The proper use of the arms is based on one of the physical laws of nature and it is in the basic pitching movements. In America today, more than 85% of the young players throw incorrectly. If their fundamental throwing movements are incorrect, we feel that someone should make a change.

434. *Is it wrong to throw sidearm?*

> Yes. We do not like to see a young person—or anyone—throwing sidearm.

435. *What is wrong with throwing sidearm?*

> If you do not make pitcher on the team, then the only other position for the pitcher is first or second base, and no other position.

436. *What type of throwing style do you recommend?*

> Three-quarter style.

437. *How about throwing overhand?*

> There is no possible way of throwing directly overhand.

438. *Is there a danger in throwing sidearm?*

Yes, let someone else take the liability for the person who throws sidearm.

439. *What is the danger?*

The elbow will be damaged if the thrower likes sidearm curves, and it is very hard on the arm or elbow to get a curve with the sidearm pitch. If the pitcher throws a sidearm or submarine pitch, there is no way the pitcher can get full power out of the front leg.

440. *What's so important about the front leg when pitching the ball?*

When pitching, the front leg supplies at least 35% of the throwing power.

441. *What about the picture called the "Finish Up?"*

This will be for a right-handed pitcher. The pitcher, or model, has spun the left leg around and has now thrown the ball and has moved his right leg around so that he can finish up his throw.

442. *Why should the pitcher finish up throwing this way?*

By finishing up in this type of position, the pitcher is ready to protect himself/herself against a hard hit ball. The pitcher can also run to either side for the grounder or a bunted ball.

443. *What does the raised leg do for the pitcher?*

It adds speed to the pitched ball, but the main thing it does is to put the pitcher into position to field the ball when it is hit.

444. *How can the pitcher practice these movements?*

Get in front of a mirror and practice these movements, such as winding up, body pivot and the step forward motion, remembering that all of it takes time to work together to make a smooth motion. When the pitcher takes the wind-up, turn on the right foot, bringing the left leg into the air, then stop and hold that position for fifteen seconds before throwing the ball.

445. *Why does the pitcher have to stop for fifteen seconds with the leg in the air?*

In holding this position, the pitcher can check his/her balance. If the pitcher falls down, then his/her balance is off. Do it again until the pitcher can hold this position.

446. On the finish-up what does the pitcher do with the right leg?

The pitcher makes sure the right leg is on the ground so he/she can finish facing the batter, ready for the grounder or bunted ball.

447. How does a pitcher watch the base runner for a stolen base?

When a base runner steals a base, it is not the catcher's fault, but that of the pitcher. Most catchers can throw the ball, but a lot of pitchers cannot throw the ball to the catcher in time for the catcher to throw the ball correctly to stop the runner from making it to second base.

448. What if there is a runner on first base, does the pitcher have to keep looking at the runner all the time?

No. The first base player will always be ready for a throw from the pitcher. Keep the eyes on the catcher. When the base runner takes a big lead off, the catcher will give the pitcher the signal to throw to first base. Then all the pitcher has to do is turn and throw.

449. As the pitcher takes the stretch getting ready to throw, does he/she have to stop for a moment?

QUESTION # 449

Yes, the pitcher cannot take the stretch and throw the ball; otherwise it is a balk. The purpose of stopping while in the stretch position is to give the base runner a chance to steal.

450. Why does the pitcher have to give the base runner a chance to steal a base?

Because otherwise the runner would not have a chance and the game of baseball would be very boring. The base runner is protected by the rule makers, from the pitcher throwing very quickly to the plate or at the base the runner is on. So make a complete stop before the stretch or wind-up.

451. *With a runner on first, is it a good idea to glance at the base runner?*

After the pitcher takes the stretch, he/she should take a fast glance at the base runner. After the glance, look at the catcher because if the runner is taking a big lead, the catcher will give the pitcher the signal to throw to the proper base.

452. *What should the pitcher do with a runner on second or third base?*

With a runner on second or third base, do not try to catch the runner off the base without giving a signal to the second or third base player so they will expect the throw.

453. *Should we figure out some sort of signal for this type of play?*

Yes. Work out signals so when the catcher gives the signal, the second base player runs for the base, and the pitcher throws the ball. The second base player should jump back on the bag to keep the runner honest. Then when the base runner gets real brave, the catcher gives the signal. This time, the shortstop will count to three and run for second base. The pitcher will count to five, turn and throw. The pitcher should catch the runner off the bag to make the out.

454. *What does the pitcher do if the offensive team has a runner on third base?*

As for the third base player, after giving the player the signal, the third base player should count to two then break for the bag. The pitcher should count to three, turn and throw. The third base player should have made it to the base by then to make the out.

455. *What should a player learn to throw before anything else to be a good pitcher?*

Learn to throw the fastball.

456. *Should the pitcher throw the slow pitch or change-up?*

Throw the change-up once in a while. In so doing, it will make the fastball look like it's going faster. A slow pitch will throw the batter's stride off and destroy the timing.

457. *With a runner on first base, how does the pitcher make a throw?*

To make a throw to first base, the right foot will pivot, and with the left foot the pitcher takes a step and throws.

When the pitcher moves towards first base, throw the ball. (This refers to a right-handed pitcher.)

458. *With a runner on second base, how would the pitcher throw the ball?*

When throwing to second base, the pitcher turns to the right as he/she pivots on the right foot. Do not turn to the left and make a complete turn. Take a half turn then pivot on the right foot. (Right-handed pitcher.)

459. *Does the pitcher have to throw the ball if he/she takes a step toward third base or second base?*

No. The pitcher does not have to throw the ball.

460. *If there is a runner on first base, does the pitcher have to throw the ball?*

As for first base, the pitcher has to throw the ball; otherwise, it is a balk and the first base runner moves to second base free and clear. So remember, ALWAYS THROW TO FIRST BASE IF THE PITCHER MOVES IN THAT DIRECTION TO THROW THE BALL.

461. *What of the picture called "Winding Up to Pitch?"*

QUESTION # 449, 461

QUESTION # 443, 462   QUESTION # 441

As the pitcher raises the ball over his head, you will notice that the ball is completely covered with the glove.

462. *What of the picture called "Raising the Front Leg?"*

The pitcher has turned on the right foot, moving it across the rubber into the dip near the rubber. Simultaneously, the left foot has been lifted high off the ground. The ball is still hidden, and the hips are turned away from the batter.

463. *What's so important about the front leg again?*

In pitching, the front leg supplies at least 35% of the throwing power, so raise it as high as possible for that extra throwing power.

464. *Why do you like the three-quarter style of throwing so much?*

More than any other type of pitching, the three Just by still play the infield or outfield with no—quarter style is the best for change-ups, fastballs andcurveballs chance, if you do not make the pitcher position, you can.Just by chance, if you do not make the pitcher position, you can still play the infield or outfield with no problem at all.

465. *What two things are most difficult for a pitcher to do?*

Rotating the hips and covering the baseball with the baseball glove.

466. *Why is covering the baseball so important?*

If the batter is smart, he/she can look at the grip the pitcher has on the ball and pretty much tell what the pitcher is going to throw—a curve ball or a fastball. So it is important for the pitcher to cover the baseball during the whole wind-up.

467. *What should the coach look for in selecting a pitcher?*

Including the size, weight and strength of a prospective pitcher, look for an ability to throw with control, and have a good fastball. A pitcher has to know how to play the position. It is not very important for a pitcher to know the curve pitch between the ages of eleven and fourteen.

468. *What if the pitcher has poor foot action?*

If the pitcher has poor foot action, he/she is usually a wild thrower. But like anyone else, a pitcher can be taught how to stand on the pitching mound and get off the mound properly.

469. Explain the picture called "Position of the Feet."

QUESTION # 469, 472

QUESTION # 473

When winding up to throw, this is the proper position of the feet. If you look at big league pitchers, this is the position in which they arrange their feet. When there is no one on base, they will take their full wind-up. Only in very special cases will they take a full wind-up with runners on base.

470. What if the offensive team has a runner on third base who is a fast base runner?

Then the pitcher is taking a big chance if he/she takes a full wind-up.

471. Why is that?

The reason for this is because if the pitcher winds-up and happens to look over at the runner at third, then throws, the pitcher has taken his/her eyes off the catcher's glove and will probably miss the catcher's target.

472. How does the pitcher place the feet on the pitcher's mound?

The right heel is on the rubber and the right foot toe is ahead of the rubber. A few inches in back of the rubber, the pitcher angles the left foot. This is the proper position of the feet. (For a right-handed pitcher.)

473. *What about the picture named, "Position of the Feet With a Runner On Base?"*

   The right foot is up against the pitcher's rubber; the left foot is in front with the toe at a 45° angle.

474. *What type of pitch should the pitcher throw to most hitters?*

   Throw the fast ball high and inside, if in doubt. This is always a safe pitch to throw.

475. *If the pitcher has two strikes on the batter, what should he/she throw?*

   If the pitcher has a curve ball, this is the time to throw it.

476. *Can the pitcher throw the spit ball?*

   No. It is an illegal pitch.

477. *What should the pitcher practice when finishing the wind-up?*

   Practice backing up the bases. When there are runners on the bases, always run for home to back up the catcher. Also, practice going behind third base.

478. *Which base is the most important to practice backing up on a hit ball?*

   They are all important, but first base is the most often used and, therefore, perhaps most important.

479. *When a hitter comes to the plate, what does the pitcher look for?*

   The batter's weaknesses; pitch to those weaknesses.

480. *How about a weak batter?*

   Never pitch a slow pitch to a weak batter.

481. *What should the first pitch be?*

   When throwing the first pitch, try to make it a strike.

482. *Where should the pitcher stand on the pitcher's rubber?*

   The rubber is twenty-four inches long and no one said the pitcher has to stand in the middle of it all the time. Move from one side to the other; that is, third base side or first base side. This could make the difference between a ball and a strike.

483. *Being fourteen years of age, what pitch should I not throw?*

   Do not try to throw the screw ball, because the reverse wrist action could cause damage to a young pitcher.

484. *Should the pitcher make the batter hit the ball?*

   If there are no runners on base, make the batter hit the ball, because if the batter is walked, it is the same as a base hit.

485. *How should the pitcher throw to the batter if it is obvious that the ball will be bunted?*

    If the pitcher thinks the batter is going to bunt the ball, pitch the ball high. That will result in a pop-up hit.

486. *What should the first pitch be on the hit-and-run play?*

    If there is a runner on first base with one out, most managers will want the pitcher to think that the hit-and-run play is in effect so the pitcher will waste the first pitch. Do not let the offensive team fool you. Put that first pitch across the plate for a strike.

487. *How many steps should the pitcher take when fielding a bunt?*

    On the finish-up, always take four steps straight forward when fielding a bunt. When leaving the mound, do not step toward third as if you think the batter is going to bunt in that direction. Move in four steps, then go in that direction when you see the ball hit there. A lot of batters are pretty good at hitting bunts by pitchers and just a little short of the shortstop and second base player. Pitchers have to cover their area first, which is the middle of the diamond, so nothing like that can happen.

488. *Why should the pitcher cover the ball when pitching?*

    Remember, few pitchers use this method of covering the ball while pitching, but the purpose of it is not to let the hitter's eyes ever see the ball until it is right on top of the hitter. It is difficult to do, but once the pitcher has mastered it, batters will not understand why they are striking out.

489. *How should the pitcher throw the ball with a runner on third and one or no outs?*

    Never throw a slow pitch. If this ball is hit, most of the time it will be hit into the air, meaning a long high hit ball giving the runner on third a chance to tag-up and score home. Throw a curve and use the low ball so the batter will hit it on the ground.

490. *Can the pitcher relax when a weak hitter comes to the plate?*

    No. Every batter on the opposing team could be the best hitter (in your mind), so throw to them thinking that way. Do not try to strike them all out. Besides the pitcher, there are eight other players on the team. A lot of pitchers relax when the pitcher from the other team comes to bat, because they think pitchers can't hit. This is not true. Never relax on any batter, even if it's the pitcher.

491. *Is the "release point" in pitching a big factor?*

Yes. In the motion of throwing, the ball leaves the hand at a certain point just after the pitcher strides. The pitcher cannot see this point of release, but it is very important pertaining to control in throwing.

492. *What if the ball is thrown low while pitching the ball?*

If the ball goes low, the pitcher is holding onto the ball too long or the pitcher has a late "release point."

493. *What if the ball is thrown high while pitching the ball?*

If the pitcher throws the ball high, the pitcher is not holding on to the ball long enough, or the pitcher is letting the ball release too soon, and the pitcher then has an early "release point."

494. *How should the pitcher throw to a batter if he/she thinks that the batter is nervous?*

Take the time in throwing the ball because the batter's muscles are tightened, and when the pitcher throws the ball the batter will be all tensed up.

495. *What should the pitcher do if he/she thinks the umpire called the pitch wrong?*

Never argue with the umpire. It will not help the pitcher if he/she gets upset. Let the manager or catcher argue for the pitcher. A good pitcher should be calm and poised. He/she should be a gentle person and never argue with the umpire's decision.

496. *What should the pitcher do while in the wind-up position preparing to throw the ball?*

Keep the eyes on the catcher's target. The pitcher will lose control if he/she looks down at the feet or at the third base line while winding-up. So, never take the eyes off the catcher's glove and target.

497. *What is a good exercise to improve the pitcher's wrist action?*

Put a ball in the palm of the hand and move the wrist back and forth like waving good-bye to someone. Doing this will loosen the forward and backward motion of the wrist and make the wrist snap a lot stronger.

498. Do you have an exercise for the curve ball?

Yes. For the curve ball, in order to get good wrist action, put your arm down at your side and then pretend you are drawing a circle (moving the wrist in a circular-type motion). By doing these exercises, you can increase your fastball by 25% and your curve ball will have a sharper break on it.

499. What should the pitcher remember about throwing the change-of-pace pitch?

That the pitcher moves the arm slowly and not the body.

500. How should the pitcher practice covering first base?

Run next to the base line with the right foot tagging the base. Always leave room for the runner and do not block the runner's path. If it seems close, slide into first base because some runners would like nothing better than to bump in to the pitcher to shake-up the pitcher or put the pitcher on the ground.

501. What should the pitcher throw to the batter when he/she has two strikes and no balls on the batter?

Do not waste any pitches. Throw as few balls as possible. The ball most batters try for is the curve ball, low and outside. That's a good one for a third strike. The low curve ball is the one most hitters do not like to be called out on.

502. What should the pitcher throw when a good batter comes to bat?

If the batter is very good, do not be afraid to put one right down the middle at half-speed. USE THIS ONLY ON GOOD HITTERS.

503. What about the knuckler pitch?

THIS IS ONLY AS A GUIDE, but one pitch out of four is good for the knuckler. Always keep the batter guessing. The knuckler pitch makes the fastball seem faster.

504. What can the pitcher do to fool the base runner on first base?

The first time the pitcher throws to first base, take a long stride. The next time, use a short stride. By doing this, the pitcher should catch the runner.

505. How does the long stride fool the base runner?

The runner has based the lead off on how fast the pitcher throws to first. So the runner will take a larger lead off the second time and then the pitcher can catch the base runner with the quick stride.

506. *How about a runner on second base?*

Only with signals should the pitcher try to catch the runner on second base. Signal coordination is required so that the second base player and shortstop know what to do.

507. *What should the pitcher throw to Junior High School batters?*

Throw the change-of-pace, but make sure it is thrown high. Usually, Junior High School batters like to stride very fast and the change of-pace will make them look inappropriate at the plate.

507A.*How would a pitcher throw to a batter who does not stride and stands far from the plate?*

Give that batter the low ball outside.

507B. *What if the batter has no stride and stands close to the plate?*

Give that batter the low ball inside.

HOW TO MASTER FIRST BASE

508. What type of player should be chosen for first base?

The player should be fairly large in size and tall so as to be a good target to throw at.

509. Is first base a hard position to play?

In baseball today, first base is not hard to play, because the ball is not bunted as much. Therefore, the first base player does not have much to do.

510. Are first base players trained on the bunt game?

No, not too many are. If the offensive team finds a player who is not too sharp on bunts, the team can bunt the first base player crazy and win the game.

511. What should a first base player practice on?

For fifteen minutes every day, the player should stand in front of the base moving each foot back and forth touching the base and also practicing reaching for the ball with the body stretched. When the player has completed that, the other players should start throwing balls to the first base player.

512. What if the first base player has a hard time reaching the ball?

Some players have this problem, along with trying to keep their foot on the base. If this is the case, have the player run out and get the ball, then move back and touch the base.

513. What if the ball is thrown high or if it is a bad throw?

For a misthrown ball, the player should be ready to move in any direction. Also, it is important to practice jumping for high thrown balls, as most first base players are weak in that area. When the ball is thrown high, the coach should tell the first base player to put both feet close together, bend the knees and jump, arms extended full above the head. For a low thrown ball, as the ball advances, place the glove still and let the ball travel into the glove. Also, be careful and avoid trying to scoop up the ball with the glove.

514. *What's the most important thing the first base player has to learn?*

How to move or shuffle the feet on the base so one foot touches the base while the other leg is used for the stretching. He/she can practice with the Strike Master and Backstop Master by placing them at the various bases to increase his/her throwing accuracy.

515. *What about the picture called "Waiting Near the Base?"*

QUESTION # 515

QUESTION # 516   QUESTION # 517

The ball has been hit by the batter, and now the first base player is waiting for the throw to first base.

516. *What about the next picture called "Moving to the Left?"*

The ball was thrown on the left side. The right foot is on the base. The left foot takes a step forward, then the catch is made. This is done very quickly.

517. *What about the picture called "Making the Stretch?"*

    The throw came from right field. His left foot is on the base; his right foot makes a big step in order to stretch without losing balance.

518. *Does the first base player throw and field the ball like the rest of the players?*

    Yes, but the first base player also has certain defensive plays that are different from the other infielders.

519. *Where should the first base player stand with no one on base?*

    About 12 feet in the direction of second base and about 10 feet in back of the base. If the ball is hit to the first base player, he/she should take it to first base for the out.

520. *What if it is a slow hit ball?*

    The first base player runs for the base and lets the second base player go for the ball. That is, if the first base player has to go far to get the ball.

521. *Where does the first base player stand if there are no outs and a runner on first base?*

    Stay on the base watching for a throw from the pitcher.

522. *What will the first base player do if the pitcher throws the ball to the batter?*

    As soon as the first base player is sure the pitcher is going to pitch the ball to the batter, he/she should run in for the bunted ball. As the first base player is moving in for the bunt, the first base player should be listening for the catcher to tell him/her whether to throw to first or second base.

523. *What should the first base player do when there is a runner on first and second base and no outs and the batter is going to bunt the ball?*

    Place yourself about 10 feet from the base line and 10 feet in front of the base. Get ready to run in when the bunt is made. Listen for the catcher to tell the first base player whether to throw to first base or third base.

524. *What should the first base player do when runners are on all the bases (first, second, third) and there are no outs and the batter is going to bunt the ball?*

    Move in to get the runner coming in toward home plate.

525. *What happens with a runner on first and one out?*

> Forget about the offensive team bunting the ball. As soon as the pitcher throws the ball, the first base player moves away from the base into the regular spot to get ready for the hit ball. If the ball happens to be hit to first base player, spin around and throw to the shortstop who is on second base. The first base player should then run back to first base so he/she can get the throw from the shortstop for a double play.

526. *What should the first base player do with a runner on first and second with only one out?*

> Get in back of the base runner and move toward the base once in a while to make the runner nervous. Keep the eyes on the catcher, because a throw may be made to the first base player to get the runner off first base.

527. *What should the first base player do if there are runners on all the bases (first, second, third) and only one out?*

> If the score happens to be close, the first base player wants to stop the runner at third base from scoring, so move in close. Now, if the defensive team (the first base player team) happens to be ahead in the score, move back farther than normal so the first base player can try for the double play, just in case it happens to be a ground ball.

528. *What should the first base player do if there is a runner on first with two outs?*

> Move off the base only after the ball is pitched. Otherwise, stay close to the base until the ball is pitched.

529. *What should the first base player do with a runner on first and second with two outs?*

> Take the position in back of the runner to make him/her uncomfortable.

530. *What should the first base player do with bases loaded (a runner at first, second, and third) with two outs?*

> Get in back of the base runner.

531. *What if there is a runner on first, no outs, but the batter has two strikes?*

> If the batter decides to bunt and fouls the ball it will be an out. But do not look for a bunt. You (the first base player) never know, so be on your toes and ready for any type of play. Do not let the batter fool you.

532. *What should the first base player be watching for when he/she receive the throw from the infielders or pitcher with a runner on third or second base?*

When the first base player has a runner on third or a runner on second, get ready to throw the ball to home plate since the runner on second might try to run home.

533. *What do you mean by the third base runner is going to "tag up?"*

This means that the runner has to stay on the base until the outfielder has caught the ball (if it is a fly ball). Once the outfielder has caught the ball, the third base runner can run for home.

534. *Should the first base player try to practice underhand throwing?*

Yes. The first base player should practice this so he/she can throw to third. Then the first base player can get the runner if the batter bunts the ball. (This is when the offensive team has runners on first and second base with no outs.)

535. *Where should the first base player be for a left-handed batter?*

Get just a little closer to first base. Then, if there is a right-handed batter, try not to let the second base player do all the work. Help the second base player.

536. *What if the catcher drops the ball on the third strike?*

If there is a runner on first when the batter makes the third strike, the batter will be out. If no runners are on base, the batter can run. If this happens, give the catcher a target 2 feet inside the base line. This way the catcher will not hit the base runner in the head or in the back with the thrown ball.

HOW TO MASTER SECOND BASE

537. *Is the second base very important in Junior High and High School baseball?*

> Yes. Second base is more important than shortstop.

538. *Why is that?*

> The reason is because in these grades (Junior High and High School), the batters swing late on the ball, making them go in the opposite field or right field (right-handed batter) so the second base player will be getting most of the ground balls.

539. *When tagging the base for a double play, is it wrong for the base runner to knock the second base player down?*

> In big league baseball, the base runner does not seem bothered if the second base player or shortstop is knocked down just as long as a double play is broken up. In little league baseball or High School Baseball, do not try this type of thing. It will only lead to trouble and more than likely end up in a fight. In big league baseball, this type of thing has to be expected and the second base player has to defend himself against such an attack.

540. *Being a second base player, what is the best way for me to touch the base without getting knocked down by the base runner?*

> The following will give the second base player excellent throwing balance at all time and is best used in Junior High and High School. The second base player will receive

the ground ball at second base. Now, when running for the base the right foot touches the base, then the second base player jumps to the right in the direction of right field and then he/she throws the ball. When using this method, it will get the second base player clear of the base runner most efficiently and is used by most second base players.

541. *What is another method for getting out of the way of the base runner?*

The second method is that the second base player receives the ground ball, touches the base with the left foot and passes over the base in the direction of third base. As the second base player touches the base with the left foot, he/she takes a step with the right foot and then throws. Now, the second base player is still in the air when he/she is throwing, because the second base player does not have the time to place the right foot on the ground.

542. *Which of the two methods is best?*

In the first method, the second base player can take a step, but in the second method he/she cannot take a step. The second base player needs a good strong arm for the second method, while in the first method the arm does not have to be as strong on the throw.

543. *What will the second base player do if he/she gets a throw from the first base player going for a double play?*

To start a double play, when the ground ball goes to the first base player, the normal procedure is for the second base player to straddle the base and give a target to the right side of the base or in the direction of right field. The reason for this is that it allows the first base player to throw to second and avoid hitting the base runner in the head or in the back with the ball.

544. *What will the second base player do with a runner on first and no outs?*

If the batter is going to bunt, stay in the regular position until the batter bunts the ball, then run over and play first base. If the second base player moves before the ball is bunted, by mistake, the batter might hit the ball in that direction. So stay in position until that bunt is made.

545. *What should the second base player do with a runner on first and second with no outs and the batter is going to bunt?*

Same as before. Move over to cover first base as soon as the ball is bunted, holding that regular position.

546. *What should the second base player do with runners on all the bases and the batter is going to bunt the ball?*

Stay in that regular position. Then when the ball is bunted, run over to cover first base.

547. *What should the second base player do with runners on first and second with one out?*

Again, stay in that regular position until the ball is bunted. Then go to first base.

548. *What should the second base player do with the bases loaded (runners at first, second, and third)?*

Get the runner at the plate if you have to, or go for the double play, giving the ball to the shortstop. If the ball is planned to go home plate, then play in a closer position by moving in a little bit so the second base player can throw the ball to home.

549. *What should the second base player do with a runner on first and two outs?*

Play your regular position.

550. *What about with runners on first and second with two outs?*

Play your regular position. The second base player can throw to any base, except home base, for the last out.

551. *What about when the bases are loaded and there are two outs?*

Play your regular position. The second base player can throw the ball to any base for the last out.

552. *What should the second base player do if a ground ball goes to the shortstop or the third base player with a runner on first base?*

Run quickly to second base, catch the ball and step on the base. Then throw to first base.

553. *What if the ball is hit to the second base player with a runner on first and second with one out?*

Give it to the shortstop. He/she will touch second base and throw the ball to first for a double play.

554. *If the shortstop is going to take the throw from the catcher when a base runner attempts to steal second base, what should the second base player do?*

> Get in back of the shortstop, just in case the shortstop misses the ball.

555. *With a runner on first and third, what does the shortstop and second base player watch for?*

> Look for the delayed steal. The second base player and the shortstop will have to develop a cut-off play. If the catcher throws the ball to the shortstop, the second base player should cut off the throw if the runner on third decides to run in for home.

556. *After covering for a bunt with a runner on first, what should the second base player watch out for?*

> Look for the base runner. After going to second, the runner will try to run to third base, or a base runner on second base will try to run home.

557. *If the catcher drops the ball on the third strike, should the second base player get behind the first base for the throw?*

> Yes. Always back up first base if the catcher drops the ball on the third strike.

558. *How can the second base player keep the base runner on second base?*

> Give the right fielder a signal, have the fielder move in closer toward the second base position so if the ball is hit to that position, the outfielder will be ready to get the ball. The reason for this is that sometimes the second base player might not be able to cover the position in time when the ball is pitched to the batter.

559. *Why can't the second base player cover his/her position in time?*

> Most pitchers in High School do not give the second base player time to get back in their normal position before throwing the ball.

560. *What about the hit-and-run play? Is it important?*

> Yes.

561. *Why is the hit-and-run play important?*

> In watching many High School baseball games, it upsets me that they do not use the hit-and-run play more often. It

would make the game more interesting and exciting. The only reason I can think of why they do not use it is because they do not know how to use it properly or how to take advantage of it properly.

562. *What is the purpose of the hit-and-run play?*

The whole reason for the hit-and-run play is to stop the team from getting a double play.

563. *In coaching the bases, what should the coach do on the hit-and-run play with a runner on first base and one out?*

The coach does not want to bunt, because the odds are not in his/her favor with this type of situation. If the runner steals, the runner is making the whole thing incorrect, because the coach will have only a runner on second with two outs if the batter bunts, or two outs with no one on base if the runner steals and is put out. So the only smart play is to use the hit-and-run play.

564. *Should the coach use the hit-and-run play with a runner on first and second base and one out?*

Yes, the coach can use the hit-and-run play with a runner on first and second and one out.

565. *What does the hit-and-run play have to do with playing second base?*

There is a large opening left by the defensive team when the runner moves. The batter will try to hit the ball through this opening.

566. *Can you give an example?*

Yes. There is a runner on first base. The offensive team has a right-handed batter at the plate. As soon as the ball is pitched, the second base player will, by normal reflex, run for the second base bag. Now, the batter can see the play, for the first base player stays on first to hold the runner and this gives the batter an opening of 60 to 70 feet to try and hit through. Nobody is there to stop the ball. The batter will attempt to hit between first and second base. Most top league teams look at the second base player moving over near the base, even though the second base player thinks the hit-and-run play is in effect.

567. *Why does the second base player run for second?*

   The second base player wants to protect himself/herself from a possible steal and does not care about the ball being hit by the batter.

568. *What if the second base player knows the batter is going to hit between first and second base?*

   If the second base player knew for sure that the batter was trying to hit between first and second base on the hit-and-run play, a signal would be made to the shortstop to take the throw for the second base player.

569. *What can't that play work?*

   This type of play is a sure blunder because a right-handed batter normally hits between second and third base. So, don't even think of trying to make that play.

570. *On the hit-and-run play, where does a right-handed batter try to hit the ball?*

   If the batter is right-handed, the batter must try to hit between first and second in the hit-and-run play, or to the opposite field.

571. *What if the batter is left-handed?*

   If the batter is left-handed, the ball should be hit past the shortstop on the hit-and-run play.

572. *Why should the ball be hit past the shortstop?*

   When a left-handed batter is at the plate, the shortstop covers second base for the steal.

573. *In big league baseball, how does the second base player and shortstop know where to position themselves?*

   In big league baseball, most of the time the second base player and shortstop know about where the ball will go because they know what pitch the pitcher is going to throw.

574. *Can you give an example?*

   Yes. On the hit-and-run play, the offensive team has no outs and a runner on first base. The offensive team has a right-handed batter, while the defensive team has a left-handed pitcher. The pitcher will throw an inside curve ball. With this type of pitch, the offensive team cannot hit between first and second, or at least it would be practically impossible to hit there. Understanding this, the third base player stays at third, the shortstop gets closer to the third base player, and the second base player moves closer to second, since the defensive team knows that the ball will go in the area of the third base line or near the shortstop.

575. *If I play little league baseball, what if the coach tells me to play second base like the big league players?*

I don't know why some coaches do this, but it is hard enough for youngsters to catch the ball, let alone run over to tag the base and then throw the ball to first base. The methods I have shown are to give the second base player a little more time to just catch the ball so he/she will not have to do all the work in addition to worrying about getting knocked down by a base runner. But remember, he/she is the coach, so always try your best.

HOW TO MASTER THIRD BASE

576. What is the hardest thing in teaching a third base player?

It is to explain to the player that there is a certain area to be covered while playing third base. Most third base players in Junior High want to protect themselves from balls hit down the third base line, so they stand only about 10 feet from the base. Then they play in too close, getting ready for bunts. Now, with this type of set up there is only a 10-feet distance for the third base player to cover. Now, the coach can see that this is where the shortstop will have to cover the 70 foot hole, and with that much area for the shortstop to cover, hit after hit will go through the this area.

577. How much area should the third base player cover?

We would explain to the third base player that more area has to be covered, at least 12 feet to the player's right or toward third base, and at least about 18 feet to the left toward second base.

578. How much will the shortstop then have to cover?

The shortstop has only 60 feet that will have to be covered for that position. This will take the pressure off the shortstop.

579. Which side should be the stronger side for the third base player?

We prefer the third base player to be strongest on the left side (second base side) rather than the right side (third base side).

580. Why should the third base player be stronger on the left side?

So that when balls ar e hit into this area, he/she will protect the shortstop's right side.

581. *Are most balls hit deep into this area between shortstop and third base?*

> Yes. When the ball is hit between shortstop and third, it is usually deep and it is pretty hard for Junior High School youngsters to grab this ball in time to throw the runner out.

582. *Where should the third base player be in case of a bunt?*

> The third base player should be even with the base and about 12 feet from the third base line.

583. *Which is the best side for the shortstop to move smoothly?*

> The shortstop will move more smoothly when going to the left side which is the second base side, than throwing to the right side or third base side. (Right-handed shortstop.)

584. *When does the third base player move in for the bunt?*

> As soon as the ball is thrown by the pitcher. This player must run in and pick up the ball.

585. *Who will call the play?*

> The play will be called by the catcher.

586. *When there are runners on first and second with no outs, does the third base player take the bunt?*

> No.

587. *Who takes the bunt?*

> The pitcher and first base player will take the bunt, with the third base player close to the base ready to get the runner on second base when the ball is bunted.

588. *Where does the third base player play when the batter is going for the big home run? (Right-handed batter.)*

> When a right-handed batter is up to bat, the third base player should be 4 feet in back of the base and 12 feet from the third base line.

589. *What if the batter is left-handed?*

> If a left-handed batter is up, the third base player should be 3 feet in back of the base and 15 feet from the third base line.

590. *Why does the third base player move over more for a left-handed batter?*

> The reason for this is to help the shortstop.

591. *What would third base players do if he/she knew what the pitcher was going to throw to the batter?*

> If the third base player is aware of what the pitcher is going to throw, then the player will position himself/herself properly. If it is a right-handed batter and the pitcher is throwing an inside pitch, then the third base player can move to the right or in the direction of third base. If there is a left-handed batter and the pitcher is going to throw an inside fastball, then the player can move to the left side or in the direction of second base.

592. *Should the third base player help the shortstop?*

> Yes. It is the duty of the third base player to protect the shortstop on balls hit into the "danger area" or the hole between second and shortstop. Also, if the ball is hit to the left or third base (toward second base) and the third base player can get the glove on the ball, then it is his/her responsibility to go after the ball.

593. *Where should the third base player play if the batter is a very strong hitter?*

> About 13 feet from the third base line and about 9 feet in back of the base. This is when a right-handed batter is at the plate. It is also important that the third base player have a good throwing arm, because the er ball will have to be thrown a lot farther to first base.

594. *What if the ball has a high bounce?*

> If the ball has a high bounce, which a lot of them do in this case, it is a lot easier to come in on the ball, rather than having it bounce over the head and having to run back to try to catch the ball.

595. *With runners on first and second, what do smart coaches (offensive team) try to do to the third base player?*

> The offensive team will try to force the third base player to move in closer so that the runners can make the double steal. The play will move the base runners to third and second base.

596. *How does the offensive team try to force the third base player to come in closer with a runner on first and second base?*

> Fake a bunt play.

597. *What if the third base player won't move in closer?*

Then when the batter bunts, try to keep the ball away from the pitcher and catcher. Get the bunt deep enough so the third base player has to come in to get the ball. This is quite risky, because a smart third base player can see the play and still turn it into a double play. So, be careful when trying this play.

598. *Tell me another play the coach can use which will give the offensive team a better chance to move the base runners safely?*

Look at the first base player. If the player is right-handed, then the best bet is to bunt down the first base line. Now, we are hoping that the first base player is in about 30 feet and a good distance from the base. Now, the second base player must cover first base and that leaves an opening between first and second. The second base player will stop if the batter can bunt the ball by the first base player as the player runs in. Therefore, there will be no one covering first base.

599. *Why talk so much about bunting the ball?*

We know that bunting is not used much anymore, but this is how to use the bunting game. Not too many coaches know how to defend themselves against such an attack. So, if the offensive team studies these ideas in bunting, they will probably drive the other team crazy. The team has to be trained in the art of bunting. If they are not, a smart team might come along and bunt your team to destruction.

600. *What should the coach look for in a good third base player?*

Third base is a busy spot in baseball, but the only requirements are that this player should have a good throwing arm and know how to stop ground balls. Playing third base is not as complicated as playing shortstop, second base or first base. The main thing to know is how to handle bunts. There also won't be as many plays to memorize as there are with the other positions.

601. *What does the third base player do with a runner on first and no outs?*

The player runs in for the bunt and the catcher will tell him/her where to throw the ball.

602. *What does the third base player do with a runner on first and second with no outs?*

Unless the ball is bunted hard, the third base player will not take the bunt. But if the third base player does get the ball, it will be thrown to second where the shortstop is playing; then the shortstop throws to first base for the double play. Remember, third base does not take the bunt. In this type of situation, the player will stay close to third base.

603. *Give me more plays in handling the ball at third base.*

There aren't anymore. The third base player just waits to receive the ball. He/she can try to make double plays when handling the ball with a runner on first base.

604. *How does the third base player prevent from getting spiked by the base runner?*

QUESTION # 604

Put the feet behind the base.

605. *How should the third base player throw the ball to the catcher?*

Keep the throw low so the catcher can tag the base runner when the runner slides into home.

606. *What should the third base player do with a runner on third base?*

If the third base player receives a ground ball and the base runner starts home, throw to home. If the runner stays on third but plans to run after the third base player throws the ball, fake the throw to first to get the runner to stay at third, then throw to first base.

607. *What should the third base player do with the base runner if there is a tight play at home?*

Move in with the base runner, keeping the baseball glove up in the air. If the ball is thrown at the third base player, he/she will be ready to catch it. Now, if a bunt is made, grab that bunt and underhand it to the catcher.

608. *Should the shortstop take fly balls hit behind third base?*

Yes. These types of fly balls are called "Texas Leaguers." It is too hard for the third base player to back up on this type of fly ball.

609. *What if a left-handed batter is going to bunt with a runner on first base?*

Move in about 10 feet in this type of situation.

610. *With runners on first and third, what should the third base player do with the base runner, if that runner is going to steal home and the catcher is going to throw the ball to second base to get the runner?*

This is called a "delayed steal" to second base. You, being the third base player, should run back quickly to third. This should bring the base runner back to third base so the catcher can throw to second base. The catcher is throwing to second to get the runner trying to steal who was on first base.

611. *With a runner on third base, a fly ball is hit to the outfield for a sacrifice fly ball. What should the third base player do?*

Point to the base runner's foot, so that the runner cannot tag up until the ball is caught. Doing this will make the runner aware that someone is watching his/her feet, so the runner will be more than careful before leaving the base to tag up. Doing this will make the runner delay, and that could be just long enough to put the runner out when a run home is made.

612. *Is that what they call a "delayed steal home?"*

Yes.

HOW TO MASTER SHORTSTOP

613. *Should the shortstop have a good throwing arm?*
     Yes.

614. *Why should the shortstop have a good throwing arm?*
     So that when the shortstop goes out to left field to get the relay
     from the outfielder, the ball can be thrown to home base.

615. *What should the player practice as a shortstop?*
     The most important thing the player should work on is
     ground balls. Practice, and more practice. When going for
     a ground ball, we have noticed that a lot of infielders,
     mostly the shortstop, DO NOT GET DOWN LOW
     ENOUGH. Again, practice.

616. *What is a good exercise for helping the shortstop get ground
     balls?*
     A good exercise is to get down as low as you can, then
     still lower, and start running. Run even faster than you
     thought you could. Being a shortstop, you cannot even
     fumble the ball for a second, or the base runner will beat
     the throw to first base. When staying low, you will find
     very few balls going through your legs, especially those
     hard hit ones.

617. *Where do the hits in the big leagues mostly go?*
     In big league baseball, a lot of balls are hit over second base.

618. *How about in Junior High and High School, where do they hit
     most of the balls?*
     In Junior High and High School, a few balls are hit past
     the pitcher's mound between second base and shortstop.

619. *How does the shortstop practice on the slow hit balls?*

When the shortstop has perfected staying low on hard hit balls, he/she should start on the slow hit ball. When practicing on slow hit balls, have the balls hit to the right side (toward third base) so when the shortstop is throwing, he/she will have the body facing first base.

620. *Is it hard for a shortstop to throw across the body to first base?*

Yes, but it is easy on slow hit balls if the shortstop moves to the right taking one, two or three steps then throwing the ball.

621. *What's the best spot for a batter to hit through?*

The best spot is, of course, to try and hit past the pitcher's mound.

622. *Where is the largest opening in the infield?*

The biggest opening in the infield is between shortstop and second base. Hitting in that area, the batter will have a better chance for a base hit.

623. *Where should the shortstop be in position with a right-handed batter?*

With a right-handed batter, the shortstop should be about in the middle of third base and second base.

624. *What about a left-handed batter?*

If a left-handed batter is up, the shortstop should be moving 5 feet more toward second base than normal. For a right-handed batter, it would be about 25 feet from second base.

625. *How far back should the shortstop position himself/herself?*

Let's pretend there is a line between second base and third base. With this line, we want the shortstop to back up about 10 feet. We do not like to see the shortstop play too deep in High School or Junior High.

626. *Why don't you want the shortstop to play deep?*

In Junior High or High School, the players do not hit the ball as hard as they do in the big league. By playing the position where we told the shortstop, he/she will have a better chance to get the balls. The batters hit mainly a slow hit ball that bounces. Now, if the shortstop knows the type of batter that is up, then the shortstop can vary the depth that will be played as well as the distance from second base.

627. *How are most infield errors made?*

Most infielding errors are made because the eyes are taken off the ball or the bounce of the ball is misjudged. So, being the coach, you want to teach the players to keep the head down longer before throwing the ball.

628. *How can the coach teach the shortstop to be more relaxed and to loosen up so he/she won't be so stiff?*

When the coach hits the shortstop ground balls, tell the shortstop before the ball is thrown to count one, two and then throw the ball. After doing this for a while, the coach will see the shortstop becoming more relaxed and more accurate in throwing and getting ground balls. With the two count being repeated, it will slow down the player's movements to the required speed and to recognize how fast the play must be to get the runner out. Also, no matter how the coach looks at it, it is practically impossible to field the ball. Anyway, the shortstop will want to get ready to throw before he/she finishes counting.

629. *Where should the shortstop be placed on balls hit to center or right center field for relay plays?*

About 33 feet from third base so the shortstop can be in position to throw the ball to second base and to stop the batter from getting a double.

630. *Who should be responsible for the base runner at second so that runner does not get a large lead off the base?*

If a left-handed batter is up at the plate, the shortstop should be responsible. If a right-handed batter is up, it is up to the second base player.

631. *What is a good play in order to keep the base runner near second base?*

The following play should be used only when the pitcher gives a signal. The pitcher will take the foot off the pitcher's rubber, facing the shortstop. Then the pitcher gives a signal with the baseball glove to indicate that the throw will be made on the "time signal count." The pitcher puts the foot on the rubber and starts counting one . . . two . . . three . . . four. At the count of four, the pitcher spins around. Now, the shortstop who counted to "three" is running for second base. At the count of "five," the shortstop and the ball arrive at the same time at the base. If the base runner is not awake for the play, or pauses for a moment, that runner will probably be out. The most important thing the shortstop has to remember is, do not let the pitcher throw the ball at all unless the "time count play" is used.

632. *If playing shortstop and the offensive team hits a lot of balls, what does that indicate about the team?*

If the shortstop is busy, the offensive team probably has a good hitting team.

633. *What are the batters doing correctly to be a good hitting team?*

The hitters are moving the bat around fast enough to hit the ball out in front. That is why the shortstop is so busy.

634. *What is the "infield fly rule?"*

The rule is not in effect if there is a runner on first base only. The rule works this way: If the offensive team has a runner on first and second with one or no outs, or the offensive team has a runner on first, second and third with one or no outs and the batter hits a fly ball in the infield, there will be an automatic out. Remember this rule, it is important!

635. *What if the base runners do not know the rule and start running anyway?*

In that case, the runners take their chances and the defensive team can put them out.

636. *Why was the "infield fly rule" made in the first place?*

Let's take an example: There are runners on first and second and only one out. The fly ball was hit to the third base player. The base runners stayed on their bases because of being afraid of having two runners on one base. The third base player, knowing this, would drop the ball on purpose near third base, then grab the ball, tag third base, turn and throw to second for the double play. As any person can see, this is not fair. This is why, in reality, there should be only one out, that being on the fly ball. So to stop infielders from doing this sort of thing, the "infield fly rule" was made.

637. *What if the base runners forget the rule?*

    The base runners will have to remember, because of the rule, that the batter will be out. Now, if the base runners do run, they will be on their own and the defensive team can put them out if they get off that base when a defensive player gets the ball, whether he/she catches the ball or not.

638. *What do they do in the big leagues when the fly rule is in effect?*

    The base runners will call out "infield fly," so the runners stay on their bases.

639. *What should the shortstop watch for with runners on the bases?*

    Watch to make sure, when the catcher throws the ball back to the pitcher, that it does not go much farther than the infield. Always be ready to back up the pitcher, just in case the catcher makes a bad throw.

640. *What if a batter is hitting to the opposite field?*

    The batter is swinging the bat late when hitting the ball.

641. *What should the shortstop do?*

    If it is a right-handed batter, move closer to second base. If it is a left-handed batter, do the reverse and move toward third base.

642. *What should the shortstop do if balls are hit past the left fielder?*

    Go out and relay the throw.

643. *What should the shortstop do if the third base player handles a bunt with a runner on first base?*

    Go over and play third base, just in case the third base player might not make it back in time to get the base runner as well as to stop the base runner on first from going to third base.

644. *What if the catcher gives the signal for a slow pitch?*

    Get ready to move to the right side, or in the direction of third base.

645. *What should the shortstop do to keep the runner on second base?*

    Keep pretending to run for second base as if to get a throw from the pitcher, for if the runner gets too big of a lead off the base there will be a score on a base hit.

646. *What should the shortstop tell the pitcher about playing shortstop or second base with a base runner on second base?*

Tell the pitcher to give the shortstop time to get back in position, because in order to fake a throw he/she will be moving back and forth. The reason for this is that the shortstop does not want to be out of position if the ball is hit.

647. *On throws from the catcher or pitcher, should the shortstop say anything to the center fielder?*

Yes. To keep the center fielder alert, tell him/her to be ready to back up the shortstop.

648. *What advice can you give the shortstop in one short sentence?*

On each play, think ahead.

649. *Should the shortstop be the one to call the outs each time?*

Yes. Also, when the pressure is on, call time out, get the infielders in a huddle, and make sure each one knows what they are supposed to do on the play if they receive the hit ball.

650. *What should the shortstop do with a runner on first and second with no outs?*

To be safe, keep the base runner close to second base. The second base player cannot do it, for the player has to watch first base in case there is a bunt. Now, as soon as the ball is pitched and the shortstop can see the batter waiting for the bunt, run in and move in the direction of third base, because the batter just might shove the ball by the pitcher who is rushing in with the first base player. If this does happen, and the ball is hit fairly hard, grab it and throw to third base. If it is moving slowly, grab the ball, then throw to first base, because the shortstop will not have time to catch the base runner going to second, since there is no one at second to throw to.

651. *What other play can the shortstop use with the situation the same as above?*

Well, if the coach likes to take chances, have the third base player cover the bunt while you, being the shortstop, cover third. If the third base player gets the bunt, which is the chance the coach is taking, the player will throw to third base and then, from third base, the shortstop throws to first base for a double play.

652. *At shortstop, am I supposed to tell the player what position to play?*

Yes. It is the shortstop's job to speak out on how many outs there are on the other team so everyone knows. The shortstop has to decide whether to try for a double play or cut-off the run at home with runners on base. The shortstop must tell the center and left fielders where they are to be placed. Then, when a left-handed batter comes up, the shortstop has to tell the third base player where he/she is going to be playing, so that the third base player can cover the open spot; then the third base player can move in the direction of second base.

HOW TO MASTER CATCHER

653. *What is the purpose of the catcher on the team?*

It is up to the catcher to signal the pitcher on what should be thrown, whether a change-of-pace, curve, or fastball. Also, the catcher will show the pitcher where the ball is to be thrown.

654. *Does the catcher signal the infielders?*

In the big leagues, the infielders look at the catcher to get the signal them on what the next pitch will be. The catcher will indicate what is going to be thrown.

655. *Who sends the signal to the outfielders?*

The outfielders receive the same signal for the second base player and shortstop.

656. *Why does the catcher signal the players?*

So the players can move in the direction where they think the batter is going to hit the pitched ball.

657. *Is this type of signaling used with High School teams also?*

No. We hope not.

658. *Why can't High School players use this type of signaling?*

This type of signaling can be very difficult for young players. First, the players could miss the signal. Second, at this age the coach just cannot depend on youngsters to hit a certain pitch in such a certain way. They are very unpredictable when it comes to hitting a ball. However, it is good to give the players signals and to prepare them for bigger leagues. This also informs them of just how involved the game of baseball really is.

659. How should I position the glove while being catcher?

Besides giving the pitcher a target, hold the glove as still as possible, and do not move the glove until the ball is near the plate. When you catch the ball, pull the glove near you so the impact will be broken. Then hold the glove still to let the umpire have time to judge the pitch.

660. Do you think moving the glove at the last second can change the umpire's mind?

With big league umpires, I do not think it makes much difference, because they are experienced in this type of movement. When they call a strike, it is called before it reaches the catcher's glove. As for less experienced umpires, it can become bothersome, especially on the low outside fastball and low outside curve ball. Some catchers in the big leagues try to pull the ball into the strike zone. In College and High School, it is quite common. The thing you are saying when you do this is, "I am going to change a ball into a strike." Then you have to argue with the umpire's decision. GIVE THE UMPIRE A BREAK. You, being the catcher, should be a friend to the umpire, not an enemy. Good catchers do not argue with umpires. The catcher should always be courteous. Umpires are human, too, like everybody else. We all make mistakes. Umpiring is one of the toughest jobs, so let the umpire make the call. Do not argue. Hold your baseball glove as still as possible until the umpire makes the decision.

661. How can the coach pick a good catcher?

In the way the player handles bunts and foul pop-up fly balls.

662. How can the catcher practice handling foul pop-up fly balls?

The catcher has to know what was pitched and how the ball is going to react when hit. It requires a lot of knowledge and instinct to do this. With a certain spin on the ball, the catcher has to know when it is fouled, whether it is going to the left or right, or just straight back.

663. Can you give the catcher some advice?

My advice to a young catcher is to throw off the mask. Then, when a left-handed batter hits a foul pop-up, move to the left. If a right-handed batter hits a foul pop-up, move to the right.

664. *Are those statements correct?*

Whether they are right or not does not matter. The main point is that at least the catcher is moving. The catcher does not pause. The catcher moves as soon as he/she knows it is a foul fly. The catcher has a better chance of catching the ball as long as he/she is moving. Just sitting there moving the head in a circle looking for the ball does not do the catcher much good.

665. *What does the catcher want to remember when looking for a foul fly?*

The thing the catcher wants to remember is to move quickly and look for the ball (take the mask off first). It does not matter which way the catcher moves, just as long as he/she moves. As the catcher moves, the eyes have a way of encircling an area in front and above the catcher. Knowing this, the catcher will have a better chance in getting that foul pop-up. Also, think about the wind and shadows when catching a ball.

666. *What if the catcher waits a second and then goes for the ball?*

The catcher who waits a few seconds will have that much more of a problem in catching the ball because of the delay. SO, DO NOT PAUSE, EVEN FOR A SECOND.

667. *How exactly, does a foul fly pop-up ball work when hit with a curve ball?*

There is overspin on a curve ball. This overspin connects with the bat, which will only get a part of the ball. In this way, the ball is not hit prop erly and will cause a foul ball. All balls with the overspin turn in the air and are difficult to catch, like a curve ball. The fouled curve ball does not go as high as a fastball.

668. *How does a fastball react when it gets foul pop-up?*

The plain fastball, which has no overspin when fouled, will not spin in the air like the curve ball. The fastball goes straighter and higher when fouled.

669. *What do experienced catchers say?*

Some experienced catchers say, "I can tell whether to move to the right or the left when a ball is hit just by seeing and hearing the sound of the ball hitting the bat."

After having been a catcher a number of years, you will be able to do the same thing.

670. *How should a catcher handle bunts?*

Some less experienced catchers run for the bunt while the ball is still being pitched. That is very foolish. Do not try it. If a bunt is properly executed, the catcher will not have anything to do with the bunted ball, because it will be too far away to handle.

671. *Do you think the catcher should handle the bunts in High School or College baseball?*

No. Let's say the catcher starts for the bunt. The catcher then has to take the eyes off the base runner or runners, with no indication where to throw the ball. In a great many baseball games, the person does not see the catcher getting very many bunts anyway.

672. *So what does the coach do?*

We have done this: Our pitcher, first base player and third base player are the professional bunt handlers and we let the catcher call the play. We let the catcher tell the players where to throw the ball for the bunt. It can work pretty well if the coach can use this method. The only other idea we have is that when the coach can find a catcher who can jump like a frog and run like a rabbit as well as hold the ball properly to make the play, the above method can be dropped.

673. *If I am the catcher and want to handle the bunt, should I use my bare hand?*

When the ball is moving away from you, as the catcher you are taking a big chance if you pick the ball up with the bare hand because the catcher cannot use the hand like a cup such as when the ball is moving toward the infielder.

674. *How should a catcher practice bunts?*

By practicing fielding grounders with the infield team, the catcher will soon get in the habit of sweeping up the ball and then throwing. Make sure the catcher uses the catcher's glove and not a fielder's glove.

675. *If there is a runner on first and third base, and the runner at first base is going to steal for second, what does the catcher do?*

With a runner on first and third base, the runner at first always runs to second base where usually the throw is never made because the runner on third base will run home for a score. This is wrong. This throw should be made, and we will show the coach how it is done. The pitcher should keep the base runners as close to their base as possible and should not be afraid to throw to those bases. Also, the runner at third will probably not run for home unless it is a close game where a run will win the game for the team. Next, pick the thrower who has the strongest throwing arm. It does not matter whether it is the shortstop or the second base player. That will be the one the coach wants to cover second base. In this case it will be the shortstop. Now, the second base player will move in about 10 feet in front of second base at an angle. The play is going to go something like this: The pitcher takes a foot off the pitcher's rubber and maneuvers to the runner at third, so that player will stay close to the base. The pitcher throws the ball to the plate. The runner on first base starts to move toward second base. The catcher throws the ball to second base. The second base player takes a glance at the third base runner and if the runner starts to run home, the second base player cuts across a place 10 feet in front of second, grabs the ball then throws to the plate to get the runner going home. Let's suppose the runner on third doesn't move: Then the second base player lets the ball go by and the shortstop takes the throw. If the runner pauses and waits, the shortstop will run that player back to first trying to get an out. But, if the runner is in the trap, the player should listen to the second base player who will call out loud to tell them if the third base runner is going home. This play is not as confusing as it sounds/reads, but if the players practice it the defensive team will be quite strong.

676. *Why can't the catcher fake toward third then throw to second?*
This is a waste of time because most young catchers just do not have the power for throwing this way.

677. *Give me another type of play?*
So you have a situation where the pitcher jumps into the air to catch the ball, thinking the runner on third will take a big lead off. Here is another one where, when the throw is

made, the second base player moves in quickly getting the throw short and rifles the ball to third.

678. *What's wrong with that play?*

All this seems okay, but usually the offensive team is ready for such a play and the third base runner stays put.

679. *What is one of the main faults young catchers make?*

With a runner coming home, the catcher waits at home plate when the throw is from the outfielders.

680. *What should the catcher do?*

Have the catcher get out there to receive the throw.

681. *How far should the catcher go to get the throw?*

It should be about 6 feet from the plate?

682. *What will happen if the catcher waits for the ball at home plate?*

If the catcher waits for the ball, it will probably get lost in the dirt and while the catcher is looking for it, the runner will crash into the catcher and knock him/her down. Then, more than likely, the runner will score.

683. *If the catcher receives the ball 6 feet from home plate, then what?*

Now, if the catcher receives the ball on the fly, he/she can run back and get the runner. We're hoping that the outfielders have been told to make the throw of the ball with one bounce. Do not tell them to get it to the catcher in on the fly, because the outfielders will usually throw the ball so high that a blind man could make it home by the time the ball reaches the catcher. Tell the outfielders to throw the ball low. In that way it will be faster, more accurate, and a lot easier for the catcher to handle. Your outfielders are not going to get this type of throwing arm without a lot of practice.

684. *As a catcher, what should I do for sore fingers?*

No matter how careful you are as a catcher, you will have bruised knuckles and sore fingers. This cannot be helped; that is part of the position you are playing. The only advice we can give you is to soak your fingers in some Epsom Salts. This will relieve the pain quite a bit. By then, you will be ready for the next game.

685. *Should a catcher be fairly large in size?*

Yes, size will help. But the throwing arm is the most important.

686. *If I am the coach, what steps should I go through to teach a catcher?*

> First, let the pitcher throw some pitches as the catcher is behind the plate. Second, put a batter at the plate but do not let the batter swing the bat. The reason the coach does not let the batter swing the bat is because the coach wants to build up the catcher's confidence so there is no fear of being hit by the bat. Third, tell the batter to swing at the ball but do not hit the ball. As coach, the thing you want to notice is if the catcher is keeping the eyes open

QUESTION # 686, 698

QUESTION # 687   *QUESTION # 688*

QUESTION # 692

at all times. Fourth, the coach can also use the Strike Master Jr. in place of the batter, if necessary. Fifth, tell the catcher that a finger will never break if the right hand (bare hand) is kept closed until the ball is caught in the glove and then the ball is trapped with the fingers. Sixth, tell the catcher that he/she and the captain will have to work together in running the team and that the catcher is going to have to use his/her brain to help the team.

687. *What about the picture, "Signal Position?"*

The catcher takes the squatting position and gives the signal. (Two fingers for a curve ball.) He makes sure that the signal is covered. The catcher places the left foot just ahead of the right foot. Some will say the third base coach or first base coach will see the signal, but if the catcher is careful, the signal will not be seen. We would put the catcher in this position so when he goes into the receiving position, he will be thinking about his feet.

688. *What of the picture, "Receiving the Ball?"*

The catcher takes this stance of about 33 inches wide. The catcher's left foot is about seven inches in front of the right foot. The reason for this type of stance is that the catcher will not have to move the feet to throw, as will have to be done on the square or closed stance in the receiving position.

689. *What are some basic signals that can be used in catching?*

One finger is the fastball. Two fingers is the curve ball. Wiggled fingers is change of pace. There is also a signal for the outside and high pitch, which is the right hand placed on the right shoulder. When the desired pitch is high and inside, place the left hand on the shoulder. For a low and outside pitch, the right hand is placed on right knee. For a low and inside pitch, the right hand is placed on left knee.

690. *After giving the signal, what does the catcher do?*

The catcher gives the finger signal then shows where the pitched ball is to go while in the squatting position.

691. *What should the catcher be aware of after the basics of catching have been learned?*

To start looking for errors in the batter's hitting. For example, taking note that "Sue steps toward the plate, so throw an inside ball," or "Tom drops the shoulders as he strides, so pitch inside and high."

692. *What about the picture in "Throwing the ball?"*

After catching the ball, the catcher should be in a straight position and ready to take a step. The hard thing about this is moving the feet. When an outside pitch is thrown, the catcher has to move to the right (right-handed batter). On pitches that get away from the catcher and go in back of the batter, the catcher will have to step to the left. Yes, the catcher has to learn the tricks of throwing. The catcher takes only one step, then brings the ball back right behind the ear, turns the shoulders, steps, then throws.

693. *What kind of a target should the catcher give the pitcher?*

A steady one. Do not move the glove at all once the catcher places the glove in the proper position.

694. *Should the catcher argue with the umpire if he/she thinks the ball is a strike?*

Never argue with the umpire. If the umpire makes a mistake, just call attention to it. Be polite and do not argue about it, or you could get thrown out of the game. Then you would be of no value to the team.

695. *How far should my legs be spread apart when catching the ball?*

Depending on your size, about 22 inches.

696. *How should the catcher receive pitches below the batter's knees?*

Catch it with the face of the glove in the downward position or fingers of the glove in a downward position.

697. *Where should the glove be placed for balance?*

Out in front of you. Do not put it close to the body.

698. *In catching the ball what should the right hand (bare hand) be doing when receiving the ball from the pitcher?*

Close the right hand until the ball is caught in the glove. Then trap the ball with the fingers. This way, the catcher will not hurt the fingers.

699. *What happens if the catcher's glove hits the batter's baseball bat?*

It is illegal for this to happen. The umpire will tell the batter to walk to first base. It is just as if the batter got a base hit. So be careful and do not let it happen.

700. *What will happen if the catcher runs out in front of the batter by mistake, thinking the ball will be bunted, with a runner on third base?*

> This is also illegal. The umpire will allow the runner on third base to score and the batter to walk to first base. This would be the same as if the batter got a base hit.

701. *What should the catcher do if a left-handed batter comes up to bat with a runner on first base?*

> Move farther back so the catcher can get a look at the runner on first base. With a right-handed batter, the catcher will not have to do this.

702. *Why do I throw wild when in a hurry?*

> Check to make sure you apply even pressure with the fingers on the ball when throwing. If the pressure is not even, the ball will go wild.

703. *What do I do if I think I can't make the throw in time to the base?*

> Do not throw. Hold the ball. If you throw, there might be a mistake and the runner will advance to the next base.

704. *To catch pop flies, should the catcher practice throwing off the catcher's mask?*

> Yes. Also, practice throwing off the mask to handle bunts.

705. *Should the catcher practice handling bunts near the third base line?*

> No. Only handle bunts near the home plate, and tell the pitcher, first base player or third base player where to throw the ball. Their backs will be to the play, but the catcher can say, "John, second base," or "Sue, first base."

706. *Can the catcher block home plate while waiting for the throw?*

> No. The catcher cannot block home plate unless he/she has the baseball.

707. *As a catcher, should I be studying the batters?*

> Most definitely, yes.

708. *If the batter is too close to the plate, what type of pitch should the catcher signal the pitcher to throw?*

> Have the pitcher throw the batter an inside pitch.

709. *What type of pitch should be thrown if the batter does not cover the plate properly?*

> Signal the pitcher to throw the outside pitch.

710. *What type of pitch is thrown if the batter over strides?*
     Signal the pitcher to throw the inside and high pitch.
711. *What type of pitch is thrown if the batter is a straddle hitter?*
     Signal the pitcher to throw the low and outside pitch.
712. *What type of pitch is thrown if the batter has a closed/narrow
     stance and steps in the direction of the plate?*
     Signal the pitcher to throw the fastball inside.
713. *What type of pitch is thrown if the batter has a "hand twitch" or
     movement of any sort at the plate?*

     If there are twitches of any kind, the catcher wants the
     pitcher to throw inside and at about the level of the batter's
     hands.

HOW TO MASTER OUTFIELD

714. *Where should the coach place the best outfielder?*

   The coach wants him/her in center field. Let me explain it again. The poorest fielder should go to left field. The next best should go to right field. We are being different than the big league players, because in Junior High and High School most of the hit balls go to right center field and that is where the coach should place the strongest outfielders.

715. *Where should the coach look for the players who will play in the outfield?*

   Look at the infield players and select three of the best players.

716. *Why should the coach do that?*

   The reason for this is that the infielders know the plays, so when they get the ball they will know where to throw the ball.

717. *Should the coach have the outfielders play the infield?*

   Yes. Try to have all outfielders play infield so they will have the experience of knowing what to do if they get the ball.

718. *Should the infielders move the outfielders if they think the ball is going to be hit to a certain spot?*

   Yes. The infielders should keep in constant touch with the outfielders. It keeps them on their toes, plus it makes them think the ball will be hit to them. The outfielders are part of the game, too, and without them the team would not have much chance in winning a game.

719. *What if the batter "chokes up on the bat" or if the batter moves the hands up on the bat?*

Move in close because the batter will not hit the ball a great distance.

720. *Should the outfielders study which way the wind is moving?*

Yes. Grab a handful of grass and toss it into the air. That will tell the outfielder which way the wind is moving. If the wind blows in the face, play farther out since this will help the ball and carry it farther. If the wind hits the outfielder in the back, the ball will not carry as far since it is going against the wind, so the outfielder can move in closer.

721. *How should the coach hit fly balls to the outfielders to give them practice?*

Try to move the ball around a little instead of just hitting flies to them. Hit them low line drives to bring them in closer. Second, hit one to their right side, then to their left side. Third, hit the ball over their heads. This will keep them moving so they can judge the hit balls. Remember, when playing in a game, the balls are not going to be hit to you. The outfielder will have to run for the ball. So when practicing, try to make each catch on the run.

722. *What should the outfielder be thinking when the ball comes to him/her?*

The outfielder should think, "Where am I going to throw the ball? I want to get rid of the ball as quickly as possible and throw it to its proper place." Plan ahead of each play or after each batter, and know where that ball is supposed to be thrown.

723. *What should the outfielder do for balls hit just behind the infielders?*

If the outfielder is in position to catch the ball, yell out, "I'll take it." If the outfielder does not yell out, he/she might run into the infielder who is running back to catch the ball. Also, it is a lot easier for the outfielder to catch the ball running forward than it is for the infielder when running back to catch the ball.

724. *I like the outfield, but I am bored. What should I do to keep myself busy?*

Watch every pitch and try to figure out how the batter is going to hit the ball, then move in that direction. Also, back up infielders when the ball is thrown to them. Talking to the batter in a loud voice sometimes helps.

725. *How should the outfielder throw the ball to the infielders?*

The ball will come in a lot faster and have a good bounce if thrown no higher than 10 feet off the ground.

726. *What bases should the outfielder back up?*

The one the coach assigns to you for different plays.

727. *How should the outfielder position himself/herself for a fly ball?*

If you are not able to catch the fly ball, make sure that it lands in front of you. It is best to get in behind the ball and come forward than letting the ball go over your head. If it lands in front of you, it will only be for a base hit.

728. *Should the outfielder pause before running for a fly ball or a hard hit line drive?*

Yes. Count to one, then go for the ball. This will give the outfielder time to see where the ball is going. Give the batter at least one base on the ball that has been hit. This way, the outfielder will have time to make the proper judgment. Do not take too many chances on balls. A base hit is not nearly as bad as a double or triple, just because you were in a hurry to catch the ball.

729. *What should the outfielder do if the fly ball is near the infielder and a catch is going to be made?*

Yell out, "You catch it, Bill," or "You catch it, Mary." This way, there will be no worry about running into each other when he/she is playing in the outfield.

730. *What should the outfielder do on hard hit ground balls?*

Keep the legs in tight so the ball will not go through them. Do not let that ball pass you. If necessary, fall on the ball but do not let that ball pass you.

731. *How can the coach teach the outfielders to throw to the proper bases?*

Use the backboard. The coach will get excellent results.

732. *What if the player seems bored in the outfield?*

    If the player seems bored playing outfield, put the player in the infield.

733. *What should the outfielders do with the ball if no one is on base and there are no outs?*

    If the ball is hit to right center or left field, it should go to the second base player as soon as the fielder has the ball.

734. *What should the outfielders do with the ball if the offensive team has a runner on first with one or no outs?*

    If the ball is hit to right center or left field, get the ball to third base as fast as possible. My advice to coaches is, do not try to get the base runner at second base, because you do not want to try to confuse the outfielders. Give them one thing to do when they get the ball and nothing else.

735. *What should the outfielders do if they get the ball with a runner on second?*

    In this case, it does not matter how many outs there are. The thing the outfielders want to remember is to get that ball to home plate fast. Do not make the decision if the ball should go somewhere else. The first base player will be close to home plate to decide whether they can get the base runner out at home or not. The first base player is also watching the base runner who hit the ball, so if the runner tries for second, the first base player can decide to cut off the throw and try for the base runner who hit the ball going for second.

HOW TO MASTER BASE RUNNING

736. *What are the requirements of a good base runner?*

    The base runner must first learn to observe the pitcher.
    Be fast on the feet and most important, THINK.

737. *After getting on base, what is the first thing the base runner should do?*

    Look for the ball. Stay on that base until the base runner
    knows where the ball is. If the pitcher has the ball, look to
    see if he/she goes into the pitcher's box. Now, if the pitcher
    does not have the ball, the pitcher will try to make the
    base runner believe that he/she is going into the pitcher's
    box. Some pitchers will move close to the box, while others
    will even make a motion that they have the ball, trying to
    fool the base runner.

738. *What exactly is the pitcher's box?*

    It is the rubber plate that is on the pitcher's mound. If the
    foot is behind this rubber, the pitcher will not be considered
    being in the pitcher's box. The foot has to be on that rubber
    to be in the box. So make sure that at least one foot is
    touching that rubber before the base runner gets off the
    base.

739. *Does the pitcher have to have the ball when in the pitcher's box?*

    Most definitely, yes.

740. *What if the pitcher doesn't have the ball when in the pitcher's box?*

    The umpire will call a balk on the pitcher and all runners
    on base get to move to the next base.

741. *How far should the base runner be from the base for different pitchers?*

For a left-handed pitcher, about 9 or 10 feet. For a right-handed pitcher, 12 or 13 feet. Of course, this all depends on how fast the base runner is at the base stealing game.

742. *What is the key point in base stealing?*

To be able to get the jump on the pitcher, or to know when to run for the next base so the base runner can beat the throw from the catcher.

743. *How does the base runner beat the throw from the catcher?*

Keep the eyes on the pitcher's feet. Now, a great many base runners will look at the hips of the pitcher, but this is wrong. If the pitcher is going to throw to first base, a step must be taken in that direction or else the umpire will call a balk. Therefore, when the base runner is watching the front foot and it moves in the direction of first base, hit the dirt and slide back to the base. Now, if the foot begins to move toward home plate, the base runner can then make a dash for second base, hoping to beat the throw from the catcher.

744. *What is the balk rule?*

The idea of the balk rule is to try to give the base runners a chance to steal a base. The pitcher is not allowed to fool the base runner or to make moves that mislead the base runner. Otherwise, baseball would be a wearisome game to watch. Now, the rule says: If a pitcher moves any part of the body, including arms, hips, feet, elbows, knees or shoulders in the direction of first base, the pitcher must throw the ball in that direction.

745. *Would there be an exception to this balk rule?*

Yes. The only exception to this rule is for left-handed pitchers when their whole body is positioned in the direction of first base and normally the pitcher will extend the arms that way as the ball is thrown. In case the pitcher moves any part of the body in the direction of the plate the ball must be thrown in that direction.

746. *What are some of the tricks that a pitcher will use to catch the base runner off base?*

Some pitchers will raise the rear foot off the pitcher's rubber, spin and throw, then take a step with the front foot, all at about the same time.

747. *What is another trick the pitcher will use?*

Other pitchers will move the head back and forth in the direction of first, never planning to throw in that direction, but to keep the base runner close to the base. Remember, bases are stolen on the pitcher not the catcher.

748. *Does the pitcher ever use the hip to confuse the base runner?*

Yes. Now, there is something to remember. A pitcher can use a hip motion, which is not a balk, because if the pitcher uses it all the time in the wind-up it cannot be called a balk.

749. *What about a left-handed pitcher?*

AS FOR A LEFT-HANDED PITCHER, WATCH AND BE CAREFUL. A left-handed pitcher can use the hip motion most effectively. This is because the ball can be thrown before the step motion is taken toward home plate. It is a great motion to have, for it can fool a lot of base runners.

750. *To be a great base runner, what should I look for in the opposing pitcher?*

We have noticed that most pitchers have a certain habit just before they throw to the plate or to first base. It is up to the base runner to study the pitcher to find out what this mannerism (habit) is, because this will give the base runner the jump he/she needs to steal the base. Some pitchers will always look to first base when they plan on throwing to the plate, or just the opposite by looking at the plate when they are going to throw to first.

751. *Can you give another example of this type of mannerism or habit a pitcher might have?*

Yes. One pitcher might straighten the right leg (right-handed pitcher) when about to throw to the plate. By doing this, the pitcher gives more of a shove-off when using the pitcher's rubber. Now, the moment that leg straightens up, that would be the time to make the run for second base.

Another example is a pitcher who has the habit of applying pressure on the front foot, and in doing this would also throw to the plate. At that very moment, make the dash for second. We say it again—bases are stolen on the pitcher, not the catcher.

752. *Should the base runner tell the pitcher about a bad habit?*

No, not unless the base runner is the pitcher's coach. When a base runner notices a pitcher with a habit, never mention it because the pitcher may change the style of pitching and the base runner would have to start all over again learning the pitcher's habits.

753. *Being a pitcher, do base runners have the same type of mannerism that will tell me if they are going to steal?*

Yes. Some runners glance at second base just before they run for the base; others lean in the direction of second base; some runners look at their feet; some apply more pressure on the left foot; and still others have a motion they go through just before running for the base.

754. *How should the base runner prepare himself/herself when taking a lead off first base?*

Keep low. Be like a dancer—be on the toes of your feet. Keep the arms stretched out, moving them up and down, so when you get ready to run you will have that extra thrust to get a quick start for the base.

755. *What do they mean by the "Stop motion" on a pitcher's wind-up?*

Let's look at the rules: When the offensive team has a runner on first base, after the pitcher makes the stretch motion, the pitcher must come to a stop. If the pitcher raises the arms and throws the ball without the "stop motion," it will be illegal. It will also stop base running. When the pitcher raises the arms, they must be brought back to their normal pitching position, then make a complete stop. When the stop is made, it can be for a second or five seconds (within a reasonable amount of time), but the pitcher has TO COME TO A COMPLETE STOP.

756. *What are the various things the pitcher can do during this pause or "stop motion?"*

>The pitcher can take the back foot off the pitcher's rubber and therefore does not have to throw to first base. The pitcher can fake a throw without it being called a balk. Also, during this pause (with a foot on the pitcher's rubber), the pitcher can spin around toward first; however, he/she must then throw to first. Or the pitcher can go ahead and throw the ball to home plate.

757. *If the count on the batter is three balls and two strikes, do you think that it is a good time to steal for second base?*

>When coaching the pitcher, we tell him/her to watch the base runner most carefully at this time, for many base runners will automatically take a big lead off the base. If the pitcher is smart, an attempt will be made to catch the base runner taking too big of a lead off the base. The only advice we can give, if the base runner does plan to run, is be very careful.

758. *What is a good saying for the base runner?*

>"If you didn't slide back to first, then you didn't have a big enough lead off the base." If the lead off is about 12 feet from the base, it is not far enough. The base runner has to get out there about 15 to 20 feet. This is a good lead off the base, but be ready to slide back to first if the throw is made.

759. *What if the pitcher is left-handed?*

>Now remember, if the pitcher is left-handed, the base runner takes only half as much a lead off the base. About 7 to 10 feet is all the base runner can take in this case.

760. *How can the base runner practice sliding?*

>Go to the nearest park and find a spot where the grass is soft and thick like a carpet. When starting to practice sliding, the base runner should wear socks on the feet so he/she will not get hurt.

761. *Why can't the base runner wear baseball shoes with spikes?*

>If the base runner wears spikes the first time out, he/she could catch the spikes in the grass and sprain the ankle.

762. *When the base runner has learned how to slide in his/her socks, what's next?*

> When the base runner has learned to slide properly with socks, look for a place where there is dirt but no grass. Wear tennis shoes this time. After that, get some sand and put it around the base about 2 inches thick and about 6 feet away from the base. Put on the baseball shoes with the spikes and practice sliding with the sand around the base. This will prevent the spikes from getting caught. Remember, first learn how to slide in the dirt with tennis shoes, and then put on the baseball shoes. Practice with the Slide Master.

763. *After the base runner has learned all of that, then what?*

> When the base runner has that down correctly, go to the normal baseball diamond and practice. Remember, to be the best at base running involves more than scoring on a long hit ball when the base runner is at first base. When working on a hit-and-run play, the best base runner knows how to make it to third. When on first base, he/she knows how to turn properly while going past second to third base. All these things require practice and more practice.

764. *Why do a lot of base runners get injured in sliding?*

> A lot of base runners take off for the steal too late, meaning that their lead off the base is only 3 or 4 feet. So, when they are stealing, they have to dive for the base head first to be safe. Now, if their lead off was about 10 feet, they would not have to slide that way, thus avoiding any injury. But no matter how careful the base runner is in sliding, he/she will get those scratch marks on the side, called "strawberries." This is part of the price the base runner pays for a good game of baseball. The sliding pads will help quite a bit, but the fun of sliding is enjoyable when he/she runs into home and the umpire yells, "Safe!"

765. *What can the base runner do for those "strawberries" or scratch marks?*

> Apply "Curity wet-proof adhesive tape" to the scratch (no bandage, just the tape) and do not take it off until it comes off by itself. If the scratch has not healed, apply another piece of tape. Do this until the scratch is healed. The tape draws the infection out of the sore. DO NOT APPLY THE

TAPE IF THERE IS A CUT. USE TAPE ONLY ON A
SCRATCH (A SCRATCH DOES NOT BLEED).

766. *What is the "head first slide?"*

QUESTION # 766

That is when the base runner dives for the base headfirst
with arms fully extended, trying to touch the base. We do
not care for this type of slide. The base runner can get
injured this way if the base player puts the glove in the
face instead of trying to tag the arms.

767. *What can you tell me about the "hook slide?"*

We like this type of slide because it fools the base player
when sliding. The base runner should work on this type of
slide. It requires the base runner to have the outside leg

QUESTION # 767

straight while the inside leg is bent or shaped like a hook.
It draws an illusion so that the base player will try to tag
the bent leg while the other leg slides into the base to
make the base runner safe.

768. *What is the "feet together slide" or "scissor slide?"*

That is when the base runner slides into the base with both feet together. It is a little different than the "hook slide." When scissoring the legs, it will remove a lot of the

QUESTION # 768

danger of the spikes getting on the back of the right foot. The same thing applies when referring to the left foot. It does not matter which side the base runner slides on, right or left.

769. *Can the base runner fool the base player with the "scissor slide?"*

No. The base runner cannot fool the base player when he/ she uses this "scissor slide." It is quite basic.

770. *Can you tell me another type of slide?*

Yes. This type of slide requires much practice and know-how. It can also be dangerous. When the base runner is sliding, it forces him/her up on the feet. We call it "hitting the dirt and coming up slide." Try it for fun if you like, but BE CAREFUL.

771. *As the ball is hit and the base runner is running to second base for a steal, what should the base runner be looking at when the second base player is getting the ball?*

Notice the second base player's eyes. The base player is looking at the ball to see where it is coming from. By doing this, the base runner can decide on which side of the base he/she may be tagged. Pick the opposite side, so the base player will have only the toe to tag. That is not much to tag the base runner with, so he/she will probably be safe.

772. *Tell me more about the "hook slide."*

This is a real good slide if the infielder runs out to tag the base runner. The base runner shows the base player the toe and one foot. Then pull it away and slide the other leg by the infielder. Or, with the leg the base player is going to tag, pull the leg away and push it under the glove. This will not work if the infielder is at the base and holds the ball at the base waiting for the runner to slide into the base. As the base runner practices the "hook slide," try to get in the habit of trying to kick the ball out of the infielder's glove as the base runner is sliding into the base. This is legal and we have seen it work a few times. Who knows? If the base runner practices at it long enough, it may work for him/her.

773. *Why should the base runner slide, even though he/she knows that he/she is going to be safe?*

Because the base runner has a great chance of rupturing himself/herself. When the base runner is running at full speed, then stops all of a sudden, the base runner can rupture herself/himself. Ask any track coach about this. When the base runner slides, he/she breaks the speed gradually so there will be no injury. The only bases the runner may not have to slide into is first base and home plate; however, at home plate, the base runner may have to slide if the throw is close.

774. *Should the base runner run at full speed when sliding?*

Yes. Start out at full speed when sliding and do not slow up for a moment.

775. *Once the base runner has started the slide, can he/she change their mind?*

Once the base runner has decided to slide, finish up on the slide even if it is into first base.

776. *How can base runners rupture themselves when running into base?*

By running into the base standing up and at full speed and then trying to stop.

777. *When the batter hits a ball for a single, what should the batter do?*

Always go around first base, and if the ball is lobbed or juggled for any length of time, run for second.

778. *If the catcher is lobbing the ball back to the pitcher, should the base runner try for a steal?*

> Yes. When the base runner is on base and the ball is thrown back slowly to the pitcher, run for the next base. Even if the base runner is on second base, he/she can steal for third.

779. *What is the key to stealing home plate?*

> Be sure to get a good jump ahead of the pitcher. Try not to be afraid of stealing home, especially if the offensive team is ahead.

780. *What else is important in base running?*

> When the batter hits the ball, run out every hit ball even if the batter thinks he/she is going to be out. Also, the batter should run as fast as he/she can, and not drag the feet.

781. *What should the base runner do on the hit-and-run play?*

> Get as big a lead off the base as you can and run as fast as you can when the ball is thrown. DO NOT PAUSE!

782. *What should the base runner do once he/she knows the pitcher is going to throw the ball to home and the base runner is on first base?*

> The second the base runner is sure the pitcher is going to pitch the ball to home, make a fast dash for second base not pausing for a second. JUST RUN!

783. *What should the base runner look for in a left-handed pitcher?*

> Be on the toes for a left-handed pitcher. THE MOMENT THE FRONT FOOT MOVES IN THE DIRECTION OF HOME BASE, DASH FOR SECOND BASE.

784. *Referring to the Slide Master, do I follow the same base stealing instructions as on questions #760 through #763?*

> Yes. The instructions are similar, except the moving ball (Swing Master) will make the player a better base runner. When the base runner is advancing in base sliding, try to kick the ball with the foot as he/she is sliding if the base runner thinks he/she is going to be out.

785. *Can I put a larger ball on the end of the Swing Master?*

> Yes. When the base runner can slide past the hard ball, then, to make sliding more difficult, use a soft ball.

HOME PLATE, PITCHER'S PLATE AND BASES

786. *What is the purpose of constructing home plate, pitcher's plate, and the bases?*

How many times have you played or practiced baseball at the spare-of-the moment without those items? No matter what kind of baseball you play, whether soft ball, hardball, semi-hard, blooper ball, etc., or just practicing by yourself, you need at least a home plate. Now, you can construct home plate, the pitcher's plate, and the bases for whatever type of baseball game you are playing.

787. *Are these the regulation sizes for professional baseball?*

Yes. The sizes of home plate, the pitcher's plate and the bases are the same for any type of baseball, professional or otherwise.

788. *How else can I use home plate or the bases?*

When you and a friend play catch, put home plate in front of each of you and practice throwing. Also, construct a base and throw the ball low, as if tagging a base runner out. You do not need a baseball diamond to practice. You can practice at home. Put them in front of the Super Strike Master and Super Strike Master Jr. to practice throwing.

789. Why should I put a base or home plate in front of me while playing catch?

> When you play any position on the infield, you are mostly throwing to a player who is on base or at home plate. For example, if you are the third base player, you throw the ball to first base trying to get the runner out. Now you have an image of the first base player and the base in your mind as you throw. So, the stronger the image the better you will throw. That is why practicing with my inventions is so important. It reinforces that picture in your mind, transmitting the information to other parts of the body, for the perfectly thrown or hit ball.

790. Why are you using plastic for the construction of these devices?

> Let me give you the advantages of plastic pipes (PVC) and fittings. First, plastic is lightweight so it will be easy to carry to school, to a friend's house or even to the park. Second, there is no need to glue all portions of the device, they sometimes hold together without glue. You can take the devices apart and put them in a small bag or carry them on your bicycle. Third, you can leave PVC outdoors in any type of weather and it will never wear out. Fourth, it is especially strong when properly supported. Fifth, it is inexpensive to use and simple to work with. Sixth, you can paint it any color and create personalized sets. These are some of the reasons we prefer plastic over any other material.

791. Can I use galvanized pipe with the plastic pipe?

> Yes. If you want more weight for home plate or the bases, use galvanized pipe with plastic adapters.

792. What can I use in place of chalk for marking the base line?

> Use any type of flour. You generally cannot tell the difference unless you feel it. Flour is an organic material, so it is good for the soil.

793. How do you construct the baseball base stations?

> First look at the picture and then the drawing. Now, cut out the various sizes of pipe and lay them out as shown in the picture. Slide them together for each station.

TOOLS FOR ALL THE INVENTIONS:

1. Tape Measure
2. Plastic Pipe Cutter or Hack Saw
3. Sand Paper to smooth the end of the plastic pipe after cutting
4. screw driver for tee masters
5. wrench for tight steel pipe (locking pliers)
6. plastic glue (pvc) where necessary

BASE RUNNER SLIDING INTO SECOND BASE

FOR CEMENT
NO SPIKES

FOR GRASS
USE SPIKES

FOR GRASS USE SPIKES

DO NOT USE ON CEMENT

Unique Bases Designs

VARIOUS HOME PLATES DESIGNS

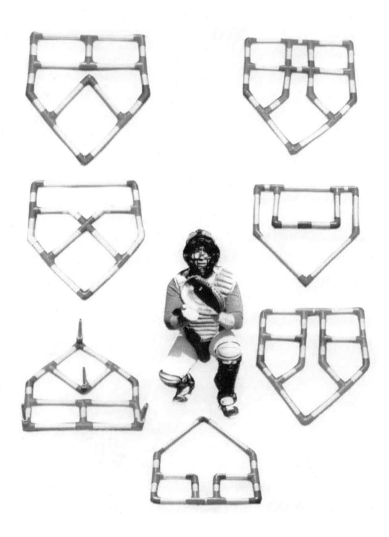

Unconnected Pipes And Fittings

HOW TO MASTER BASEBALL   © LEWY

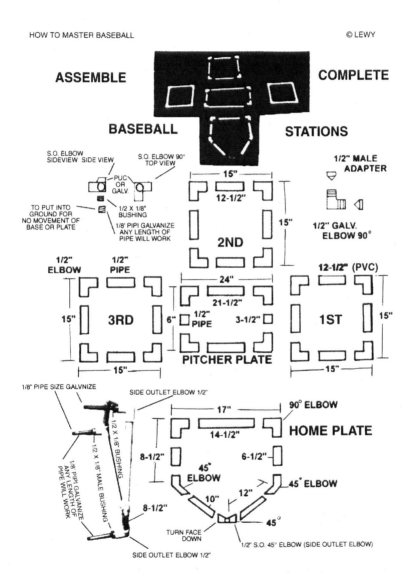

ASSEMBLE

COMPLETE

BASEBALL

STATIONS

S.O. ELBOW
SIDEVIEW SIDE VIEW

S.O. ELBOW 90°
TOP VIEW

PUC
OR
GALV.

TO PUT INTO
GROUND FOR
NO MOVEMENT OF
BASE OR PLATE

1/2 X 1/8"
BUSHING

1/8' PIPI GALVANIZE
ANY LENGTH OF
PIPE WILL WORK

1/2" MALE
ADAPTER

15"

12-1/2"

15"

2ND

1/2" GALV.
ELBOW 90°

1/2"
ELBOW

1/2"
PIPE

24"

21-1/2"

12-1/2" (PVC)

15" **3RD**

6" **1/2"**
PIPE

3-1/2"

1ST   15"

15"

PITCHER PLATE

15"

1/8" PIPE SIZE GALVNIZE

SIDE OUTLET ELBOW 1/2"

1/2 X 1/8" BUSHING

1/8' PIPI GALVANIZE
ANY LENGTH OF
PIPE WILL WORK

1/2 X 1/8" MALE BUSHING

8-1/2"

8-1/2"

SIDE OUTLET ELBOW 1/2"

17"

14-1/2"

90° ELBOW

HOME PLATE

6-1/2"

45°
ELBOW

10"

12"

45° ELBOW

45°

TURN FACE
DOWN

1/2" S.O. 45" ELBOW (SIDE OUTLET ELBOW)

STANCE AND STRIDE DEVICE

794. *What is the Stance and Stride Device?*

It is a device that will give the batter the proper stance and stride while hitting the ball. With this device, the batter cannot stride more than 7 inches. It gives the batter a perfectly controlled stride for his/her hitting (question #120).

795. *What is the 45° elbow used for when starting the stance?*

The 45° elbow is optional on this device. It can be used by a batter who is not sure whether he/she is placing the front foot at a 45° angle when in the stance position. Once the batter has adapted to keeping that 45° angle, he/she can remove it.

796. *Should I use 1/2-inch or 3/4-inch plastic pipe and fittings?*

You can use either one, but for additional weight when hitting a pitched ball, use galvanized fittings at certain locations of the plate. For example, at the end or corners of the plate use a 1/2-inch or 3/4-inch galvanized side outlet elbow with plastic male adapters. First, screw a 2-inch or longer galvanized nipple into the side outlet elbow, turning it face down. Second, push the nipple into the ground so the plate will not move. Remember, the 1/2-inch galvanized fittings are lighter, so you can carry it to school or a friend's house. Whereas, the 3/4-inch fittings are heavier, making the device not feasible for portability.

797. What is the widest stance the batter can get with this device?
As on the drawing, 20 inches is the widest the batter can stand. For a wider stance, cut the pipes longer, remembering to put equal balance on both feet. Also, drill some holes and put in a pin, or use a spring clamp, so the stance can be adjusted without moving. This will prevent the back foot from veering backward as the batter pivots. Use the thinnest gauge (3/4-inch) pipe to slide over the 1/2-inch pipe for adjusting to the proper stance.

798. How does a person construct the Stance and Stride Device?
Look at the picture. It will give you a side view of the device taken apart. The front view is the device fully assembled. There is also a top view in the drawing. Cut out the pipe sizes and lay them as shown in the picture. Put all the fittings and pipe sizes together and you will have the Stance and Stride Device for a lifetime of practice.

799. How do you bat left handed with the Stance and Stride Device?
All the batter has to do is turn the Stance and Stride Device over, then he/she can be a "switch hitter" (a batter who can hit left or right-handed).

STANCE AND STRIDE DEVICE
UNCONNECTED PIPES AND FITTINGS

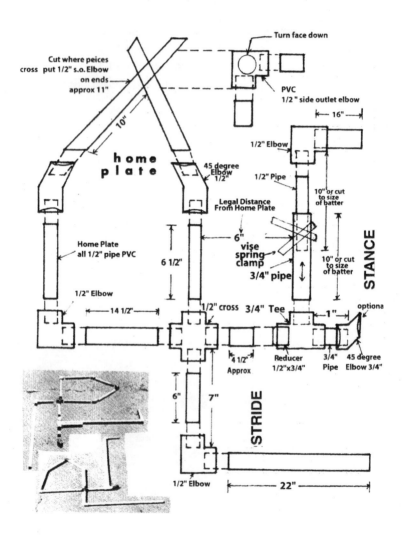

Turn face down

Cut where peices cross put 1/2" s.o. Elbow on ends approx 11"

PVC
1/2 " side outlet elbow

16"

1/2" Elbow

1/2" Pipe

10" or cut to size of batter

10"

h o m e
p l a t e

45 degree Elbow 1/2"

Legal Distance From Home Plate

6"
vise spring clamp

3/4" pipe

10" or cut to size of batter

STANCE

Home Plate all 1/2" pipe PVC

6 1/2"

1/2" Elbow

14 1/2"

1/2" cross   3/4" Tee

1"

optiona

Reducer 1/2"x3/4"

3/4" Pipe

45 degree Elbow 3/4"

4 1/2" Approx

6"   7"

STRIDE

1/2" Elbow

22"

TEE MASTERS

800. Why are the pictures of the Tee Master shown in a plastic model?

Because the player can construct the Tee Master in plastic or galvanized pipe, whichever he/she prefers.

801. Which one do you recommend for using as a Tee Master?

We recommend any of them. However, construct it with a base of galvanized pipe. In starting out, the object is to have a heavy base, but not so heavy that it is difficult to maneuver for carrying with you to school or to a friend's house.

802. Do you like the Tee Master that is demonstrated in the book as a batting apparatus?

Yes. It is easy to make and has a good base.

803. Can we make our own model of the Tee Master?

Yes. I have designed about 27 models to get you started.

804. What are the classifications of advancements?

Use this only as a guide: First, we want the batter to start with a softball for hitting only if he/she is having a difficult time hitting a hard ball. Second, we want the batter to use a larger rubber hose about 7/8-inch or larger in diameter to go over the 3/4-inch height pole (thick gauge) plastic pipe with a hose clamp. The hose clamp will prevent the hose from coming off the height pole when hitting the ball. The rubber hose should be about 7 inches or longer in length. To start, when the batter can do all the hitting without bumping down the Tee Master—low pitch, knee pitch or high pitch, plus inside, outside, or middle—the batter is ready for the next step. (Note: The batter must be hitting the hard ball as strong as he/she can before going on to the next phase.) Third, use the plastic base with 3/4-inch pipe and a small plastic tip for holding the ball (such as a 3/4-inch x 1-inch tip) if the batter prefers. Now, when the batter can hit the ball without knocking down the Tee Master, he/she is at the stage of a CHAMPION IN THE ART AND SCIENCE OF HITTING.

805. *Can the batter get any better than that?*

Yes. To check if the batter has become a GRAND MASTER IN THE ART AND SCIENCE OF HITTING, build the Tee Master the following way: Use a very small base, like a 1-inch sleeve with 1/2-inch plastic pipe, and a 1/2-inch sleeve for a tip. Now, if the batter can hit the ball without shoving, or touching, the Tee Master and hitting the ball into the air and out of the infield (depending on age), then he/she can consider himself/herself a GRAND MASTER IN THE ART AND SCIENCE OF HITTING FOR THAT HOME RUN BALL.

806. *Can we play games using the Tee Master?*

Yes. Each person, at his/her own stage, can challenge another person. Remember, when you are playing this way, it is a game. Some are good on the high pitch balls, while others are good on the low pitch balls. Keep in mind, we want to have fun playing. Do not laugh and tease a person if he/she misses. When using the tee, it is a difficult type of batting game. IT WILL TAKE CONSIDERABLE PATIENCE, EXTENSIVE WORK AND RIGOROUS PRACTICE TO MASTER THE BATTING TEE OR TEE MASTER PROPERLY. THEREFORE, EACH PERSON MUST ADVANCE AT HIS/HER OWN PACE. To start, we recommend a little practice each day. *THE MAIN THING TO THINK UPON IS THAT YOU DON'T GIVE UP; KEEP PLAYING BASEBALL NO MATTER WHAT YOUR LEVEL OF HITTING.* We play baseball to have fun and enjoyment, so everyone can play baseball at any level.

807. *How can we play a game and what might the rules be?*

I call it the BATTING MASTER GAME. First, each player must have the same kind of Tee Master or one Tee Master with each of his/her own height level poles of plastic pipes—high, middle, low. Second, each person will complete every section, hitting up against the Backstop Master, Bat Speed apparatus or a chain link fence (just as a warm up). Now, use the Low Tee Master and work up to the High Tee Master. Move the Tee Master at each stage. The first stage—outside low, middle low, and low inside—is equal to one section. Then, each time the Tee Master is knocked down or you don't hit the Backstop Master on a direct fly ball, the batter will lose a point. For example, low outside, low middle, low inside, waist outside, waist middle, waist inside, shoulder outside, shoulder middle and shoulder inside (note: shoulders, or to make it legal, arm-pit level) is one complete round, or nine points. The batter will alternate hitting the ball after one section. Then the next batter is up to hit the ball. Play three or more complete rounds for a total of 27 points. Also, alternate after each section and the next person hits the ball. If you can, make it similar to a baseball game using many variations of playing. Give a penalty to a person that is older than you or is at a higher level of hitting than you are so you will both have an equal challenge. Try to make the rules very simple.

808. *What if I have a hard time moving to another level?*

We believe that with the Tee Master and with all the inventions, you will have a difficult time at the start. However, we repeat: IT WILL TAKE CONSIDERABLE PATIENCE, EXTENSIVE WORK AND RIGOROUS PRACTICE TO MASTER THE TEE MASTER PROPERLY. EACH PERSON MUST MOVE AT HIS/HER OWN PACE. THE MAIN THING TO THINK UPON IS THAT YOU DON'T GIVE UP; KEEP PLAYING BASEBALL NO MATTER WHAT YOUR LEVEL OF HITTING.

809. *What if we have a tie score and no one knocked down the Tee Master?*

That is very good. You should now move back from the Bat Speed Apparatus, Backstop Master or fence to get a greater distance away. If the batter misses the fence by not hitting the ball hard enough, so that it goes on the ground, the batter loses a point (do not forget about penalty players). If the batter hits off the Tee Master but does not hit the fence with the ball going in the air, the batter will lose a point. If the batter knocks down the Tee Master plus misses the fence, he/she loses two points. Keep moving the Tee Master back away from the fence until you have a winner.

810. *How can I figure my batting average like the professionals?*
Let's use the following example: You have been at bat 86 times and hit safely 39 times. Using your calculator, first press 39 for the number of base hits. Second, press the divide sign. Third, press 86 for the number of times you were at bat. Fourth, hit the equal sign (=) to finish your calculation. The result will be a batting average of .45348 or .453 rounded off. You have 39 base hits and were put out 47 times which give you a total of 86 times at bat. Here's another example:

$$39 \text{ for } 86 = 453 \text{ Batting average} = \frac{\text{Number of Base Hits}}{\text{Time At Bat}}$$

OR: Batting average =   .45348 (or .453)
     Times at Bat   86)39.0000—Number of Base Hits
                        34.4xxx
                         4.60
                         4.30
                          .300
                          .258
                          420
                          344
                          760
                          688
                           72

Tee Master

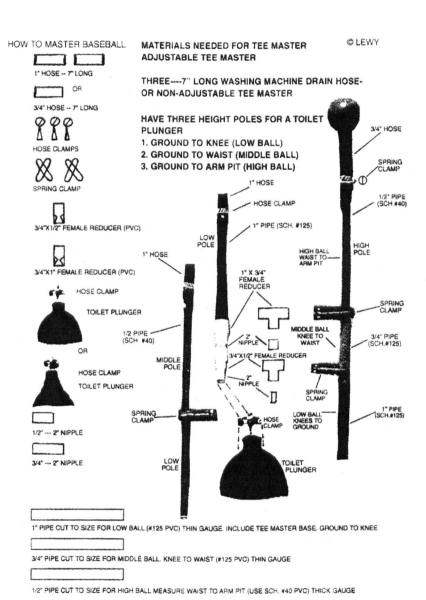

HOW TO MASTER BASEBALL

1" HOSE -- 7" LONG

OR

3/4" HOSE -- 7" LONG

HOSE CLAMPS

SPRING CLAMP

3/4"X1/2" FEMALE REDUCER (PVC)

3/4"X1" FEMALE REDUCER (PVC)

HOSE CLAMP

TOILET PLUNGER

OR

HOSE CLAMP

TOILET PLUNGER

1/2" --- 2" NIPPLE

3/4" --- 2" NIPPLE

MATERIALS NEEDED FOR TEE MASTER
ADJUSTABLE TEE MASTER

© LEWY

THREE----7" LONG WASHING MACHINE DRAIN HOSE-
OR NON-ADJUSTABLE TEE MASTER

HAVE THREE HEIGHT POLES FOR A TOILET
PLUNGER
1. GROUND TO KNEE (LOW BALL)
2. GROUND TO WAIST (MIDDLE BALL)
3. GROUND TO ARM PIT (HIGH BALL)

1" HOSE

HOSE CLAMP

1" PIPE (SCH. #125)

LOW POLE

1" HOSE

1/2 PIPE (SCH. #40)

MIDDLE POLE

SPRING CLAMP

LOW POLE

1" X 3/4" FEMALE REDUCER

2" NIPPLE

3/4"X1/2" FEMALE REDUCER

2" NIPPLE

MIDDLE BALL KNEE TO WAIST

HOSE CLAMP

LOW BALL KNEES TO GROUND

SPRING CLAMP

TOILET PLUNGER

3/4" HOSE

SPRING CLAMP

1/2" PIPE (SCH. #40)

HIGH BALL WAIST TO ARM PIT

HIGH POLE

SPRING CLAMP

3/4" PIPE (SCH. #125)

1" PIPE (SCH. #125)

1" PIPE CUT TO SIZE FOR LOW BALL (#125 PVC) THIN GAUGE. INCLUDE TEE MASTER BASE. GROUND TO KNEE

3/4" PIPE CUT TO SIZE FOR MIDDLE BALL. KNEE TO WAIST (#125 PVC) THIN GAUGE

1/2" PIPE CUT TO SIZE FOR HIGH BALL MEASURE WAIST TO ARM PIT (USE SCH. #40 PVC) THICK GAUGE

VARIOUS TEE MASTERS
UNCONNECTED FITTINGS

HOW TO MASTER BASEBALL

©LEWY
2002

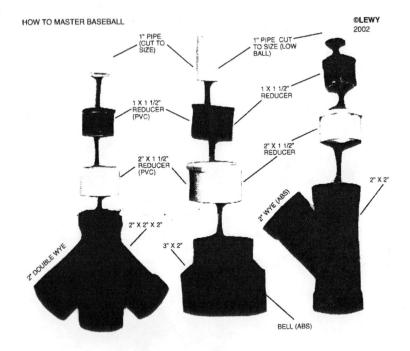

1" PIPE
(CUT TO
SIZE)

1" PIPE CUT
TO SIZE (LOW
BALL)

1 X 1 1/2"
REDUCER

1 X 1 1/2"
REDUCER
(PVC)

2" X 1 1/2"
REDUCER

2" X 1 1/2"
REDUCER
(PVC)

2" X 2"

2" WYE (ABS)

2" X 2" X 2"

2" DOUBLE WYE

3" X 2"

BELL (ABS)

CONNECTED PIPES AND FITTINGS

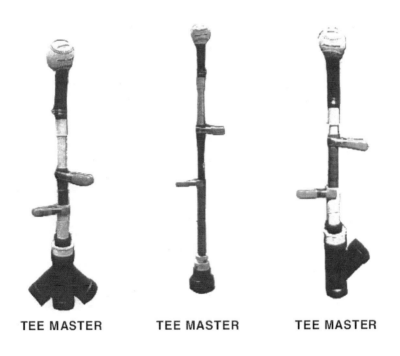

TEE MASTER   TEE MASTER   TEE MASTER

ASSORTED TEE MASTERS

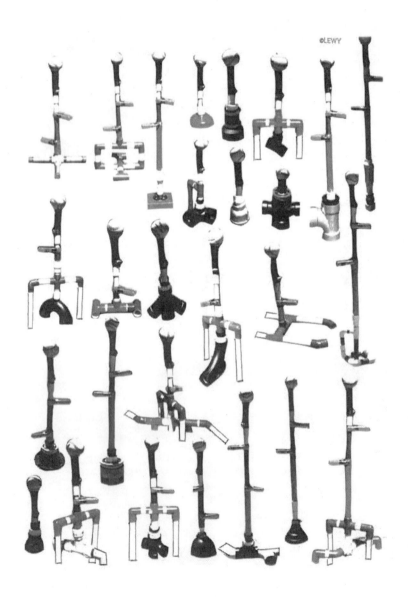

BAT MASTER

811. *What is the Bat Master?*

The Bat Master does the same thing as the Tee Master, but the Bat Master is more precise and less awkward when moving the height pole. The batter does not have to figure out where the various pitches will be placed as he/she does with the Tee Master. The Bat Master is the Stance and Striding Device plus the Tee Master all in one apparatus. It is more accurate and once the apparatus is set up, it need not be moved for various pitches, as with the Tee Master. Remember, the Bat Master stops the ball where it should be hit, just like the Tee Master does. Also, even though the ball is not moving, it is at the exact point in time when the flight of the ball and the swinging of the bat make contact. The thing the batter wants to think about while practicing is getting the "Hit Area"—or barrel of the bat—to make contact with the ball, while the ball is in flight, for that home run.

812. *Explain the picture Full Plate Coverage.*

This is for the proper plate coverage for all balls being hit (refer to Question #65). The design of the Bat Master requires the batter to stay the legal distance away form the plate, which is six inches when the batter is hitting the ball. In this manner, the batter will not get hit by the pitched ball because he/she is too close to the plate.

813. *Explain the picture "Ready At The Plate." (Question #85.)*

    This is how the batter should stand when he/she is ready to hit the ball. If playing a game, by removing the center portions of the Bat Master, it will look similar to the Stance and Stride Device.

814. *Will the Bat Master fit any size batter?*

    Yes. No matter what size the batter is, the Bat Master should fit the swing, as long as the batter uses the appropriate methods of proper plate coverage. The only thing different is each person should have his/her own Tee Height Poles.

815. *Can the batter practice alone with the Bat Master?*

    Yes. If the player has constructed the Bat Speed Apparatus or the Backstop Master, then position the Bat Master in front of the apparatus for your hitting practice. As you notice each picture for hitting, look only at where the Tee Height pole is placed in the Bat Master.

816. *I want to hit left-handed, is there anything I have to change on the Bat Master?*

    No, the Bat Master was invented for the left-handed or right-handed batter. All the batter has to do is move to the other side of the plate; it is identical for either side. It is excellent for practicing "switch hitting" (batting left or right-handed).

817. *Do you feel a batter should have a warm-up time before going to bat?*

    Yes, but up until now, the batter had no way to practice before going to bat. Therefore, with my inventions, we feel, during a baseball game, the players who are batting third and fourth should be practicing on the Bat Master or Tee Master before he/she goes to bat. This would be an excellent way to improve their hitting. Also, this is one of the many reasons why we have so many deplorable hitters. They do not have the proper warm-up time before hitting the ball when going to bat.

818. *Do you think the Bat Master will help coaches pick the best hitters?*

    Yes, it will help the coaches pick the best players in hitting. The coach can find out what stage of the Tee Master or

Bat Master the batter is at and give him/her the final test.
Make the Bat Master out of galvanized pipe and plastic
pipe and fittings to see who will be the best hitters.

819. *Do you think it will help the coaches pick a good "pinch hitter,"
when a game is close or in the last inning?*

Yes. Let's look at an example of the "pinch hitter" (a player
who will take the place of the regular batter). It is a close
game. Will the pinch hitter be ready? Give the batter a
quick test on the Bat Master/Tee Master to make sure
his/her form is working properly; if not, then try another
pinch hitter. This will tell the coach at a glance if the batter
is hitting properly for that day, or before the coach brings
him/her into the game.

820. *Can I make the Bat Master out of all plastic pipe and fittings?*

Yes, but we recommend a little of both plastic pipes and
some galvanized fittings. Use 1/2-inch pipes and fittings
for easy portability.

821. *What if I use 3/4-inch pipes and fittings made of all galvanized
pipes as shown in the drawing?*

It will not be good for transporting. It might be excellent
for schools, parks and your backyard if you do not move
it too much. Now, you have a non-wearable apparatus for
adults and children to use for many years.

822. *Explain the picture "High Outside, Bat Master."*

Place your Tee High Height Pole in the outside corner of
the Bat Master. Now, with any high pitched ball, take the
Horizontal swing. It will be the same as Picture #261 or
Question #261 with the Tee Master. That is the proper way
to swing the bat.

823. *What about the measurements of the placing of the height
pole to the outside ball, middle ball, inside ball, are those
distances for my height?*

Yes, make sure the player has the proper plate coverage.
Also, the longer the bat or your arms, the farther away
from the plate you will stand. The line of swing should be
the same, whether the batter is a short or a tall person,
and no matter what length of baseball bat the batter may
use.

824. *What about the picture "Waist High Outside?"*

> Any waist high pitch takes the half-horizontal swing. You should refer to Pictures and Questions #212 and #224.

825. *What about the picture "Low Inside?"*

> With any low pitch ball, the batter should swing the bat at three-quarter horizontal. You should refer to Question #251 for proper swing.

826. *What's the picture "Waist High Inside and Waist High Middle?"*

> It is the same as with the rest of the pictures, except you have a front view of the Bat Master. Refer to Questions #230 and #222 for hitting the ball with the Half Horizontal swing using the Tee Master.

827. *What about the picture "Vertical Swing For Below the Knee Ball?"*

> The height pole is measured for balls just a little below the knees. It is just in front of the middle ball on the Bat Master. Refer to Picture and Question #146 for the proper way to swing the bat for the Vertical Swing. Remember, this is not a strike ball, but an umpire could call it a strike. That is why I put it on the Bat Master. Using the Vertical Swing is the only swing that can hit a pitched ball that low properly for a home run.

828. *What of the picture called the Bat Master Number Identification?*

> This is a top view of the Bat Master. It clarifies things a little better about the Bat Master.

829. *How does a person construct the Bat Master?*

> It is basically the same as the Stride and Stance Device, except you will put tees between the width of the plate, which is 3 tees, plus the lengths of the pipe. Add more tees to connect with them, showing face-up, for your height pole to be placed into.

830. *Are the measurements the same for galvanized pipe and plastic pipe?*

> Yes, the lengths will be quite similar, but note adjustments for adapters, making the pipe shorter than they should be. When no plastic male adapters are used, plastic pipes will be about the same as galvanized pipes.

831. Can I use all plastic pipe and fittings for the Bat Master?
Yes. The drawing is for a permanent type of Bat Master, because the 3/4-inch galvanized pipes and fittings are heavy. We suggest a person try 1/2-inch pipes and fittings for easier portability. There are so many various ways of assembling the Bat Master to fit your special needs.

BAT MASTER WITH FULL PLATE COVERAGE

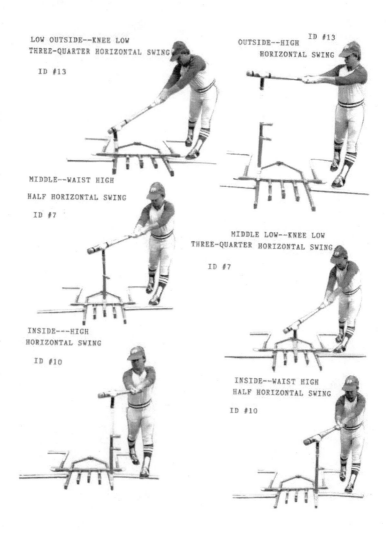

LOW OUTSIDE--KNEE LOW
THREE-QUARTER HORIZONTAL SWING

ID #13

OUTSIDE--HIGH
HORIZONTAL SWING
ID #13

MIDDLE--WAIST HIGH
HALF HORIZONTAL SWING
ID #7

MIDDLE LOW--KNEE LOW
THREE-QUARTER HORIZONTAL SWING
ID #7

INSIDE---HIGH
HORIZONTAL SWING
ID #10

INSIDE--WAIST HIGH
HALF HORIZONTAL SWING
ID #10

BAT MASTER WITH FULL PLATE COVERAGE

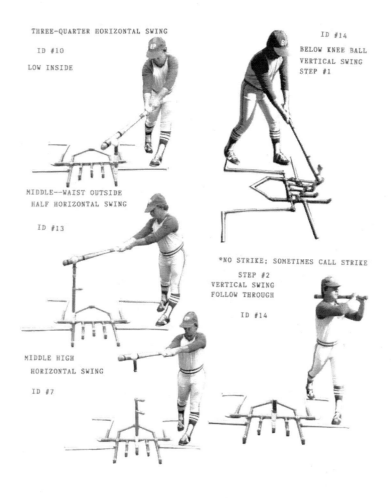

THREE-QUARTER HORIZONTAL SWING

ID #10

LOW INSIDE

ID #14

BELOW KNEE BALL
VERTICAL SWING
STEP #1

MIDDLE--WAIST OUTSIDE
HALF HORIZONTAL SWING

ID #13

*NO STRIKE; SOMETIMES CALL STRIKE

STEP #2
VERTICAL SWING
FOLLOW THROUGH

ID #14

MIDDLE HIGH
HORIZONTAL SWING

ID #7

Bat Master With Full Plate Coverage

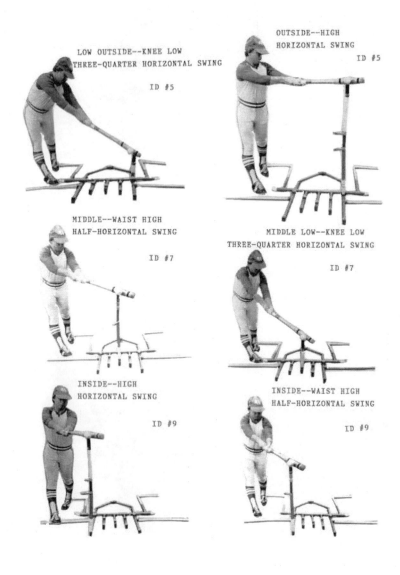

LOW OUTSIDE--KNEE LOW
THREE-QUARTER HORIZONTAL SWING

ID #5

OUTSIDE--HIGH
HORIZONTAL SWING

ID #5

MIDDLE--WAIST HIGH
HALF-HORIZONTAL SWING

ID #7

MIDDLE LOW--KNEE LOW
THREE-QUARTER HORIZONTAL SWING

ID #7

INSIDE--HIGH
HORIZONTAL SWING

ID #9

INSIDE--WAIST HIGH
HALF-HORIZONTAL SWING

ID #9

UNCONNECTED PIPES AND FITTINGS

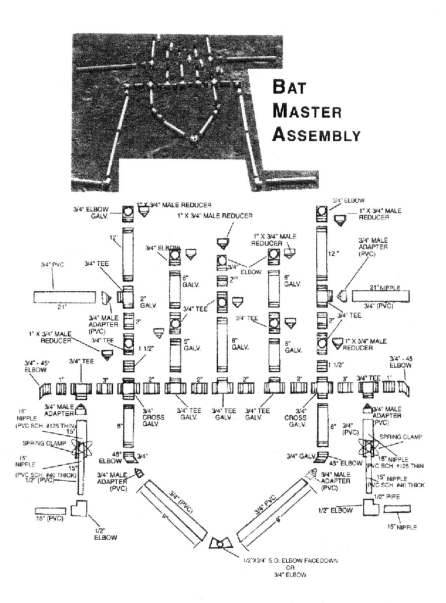

BAT
MASTER
ASSEMBLY

Bat Master Number Identification

© LEWY

1. STANCE FOR RIGHT HANDED BATTER
2. STRIDE FOR RIGHT HANDED BATTER
3. STANCE FOR LEFT HANDED BATTER
4. STRIDE FOR LEFT HANDED BATTER
5. OUTSIDE BALL FOR LEFT HANDED BATTER
6. OUTSIDE MIDDLE BALL FOR LEFT HANDED BATTER
7. MIDDLE BALL FOR LEFT/RIGHT HANDED BATTER
8. INSIDE MIDDLE BALL FOR LEFT HANDED BATTER
9. INSIDE BALL FOR LEFT HANDED BATTER
10. INSIDE BALL FOR RIGHT HANDED BATTER
11. INSIDE MIDDLE BALL FOR RIGHT HANDED BATTER
12. OUTSIDE MIDDLE BALL FOR RIGHT HANDED BATTER
13. OUTSIDE BALL FOR RIGHT HANDED BATTER
14. VERTICAL SWING FOR BELOW THE KNEE BALL (NO STRIKE)
FOR RIGHT/LEFT HANDED BATTER (VERY CLOSE TO STRIKE ZONE)

15. STRIDE STOP BAR RT. HANDED BATTER
16. STRIDE STOP BAR LT. HANDED BATTER
17. HOME PLATE
18. 45°ANGLE FOR FRONT FOOT RT. HANDED BATTER
19. 45°ANGLE FOR FRONT FOOT LT. HANDED BATTER
20. ADJ. STOP BAR FOR BACK FOOT RT. HANDED BATTER
21. ADJ. STOP BAR FOR BACK FOOT LT. HANDED BATTER
22. ADJ. STANCE SPRING CLAMPS LOCK
23. LEGAL DISTANCE FROM HOME PLATE

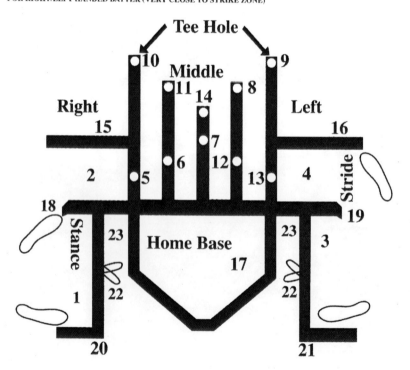

BAT SPEED APPARATUS

832. *What is the Bat Speed Apparatus?*

The Bat Speed Apparatus is many things pertaining the Art and Science of Baseball Practice. We feel it is the most important and convenient way to practice baseball by yourself to improve your hitting and throwing without two or three players to help, as you will notice this in the picture for the throwing exercise. Place a sheet of wood with the strike zone painted on it against the Bat Speed Apparatus. Sit in a chair as described in the throwing chapter (Question #358) for more wrist and forearm speed. Notice the picture for proper bat speed practice (Question #173). Do the exercise for those extra quick hands for complete hand control. Notice the picture, for you can use the Tee Master, Bat Master, or the Stance and Striding Device for this practice exercise in hitting. For throwing various pitches, use the Stepping Square for throwing the ball.

833. *Does the Bat Speed Apparatus work well in a small area?*

We designed the apparatus for a small area, like a garage, or even a room in the house. Who would have thought that you could practice baseball in the house? The apparatus will fit into any area of approximately 8 feet wide, 6 feet deep, and 7 feet high (after removing the top section of the backboard, if necessary). So, now the player will always be in fit for baseball no matter what the season.

834. What if the batter is left-handed?

The only thing the batter will have to do different is reverse the top cross bar which supports the ball, and reverse the side of the apparatus. Then it is ready for a left-handed batter. This pertains to all my inventions. The player can practice with them batting or throwing left handed or right handed. As for batting, the hitter can be the perfect "switch hitter."

835. What is so important about the instructions?

We want you to read the instructions at least once before you start construction. It is simple to construct, but you should read the instructions before you start. Then take each step one at a time. DO NOT GET IN A HURRY, FOR ALL GOOD THINGS TAKE TIME.

836. What is the first step in constructing the Bat Speed Apparatus?

You will have to purchase 1-inch PVC (thick gauge) and fittings for this batting apparatus. Next, you will need approximately 11 (eleven) 10-foot lengths of 1-inch plastic pipe. Cut the lengths of the pipe with a hacksaw. Materials needed for construction: you will need 1 pipe cut to a length of 100 inches (compare drawing to Step #1) and 1 piece of pipe cut to a length of 78 inches, until all pipe lengths are cut down to 8-inch lengths of pipe. Remember to mark each pipe. This is so you will not have to re-measure if the pipes get mixed up.

837. What is the second step of construction?

You must station the base or foundation as shown in Step #1. The layout of the pipes in the drawing and pictures are similar. Now, in the drawing where it says TOP VIEW BASE, the section inside the foundation is what goes on the top, over the batter's head, where the ball hangs down. That is not part of the foundation. Connect all foundation pipes and fittings, starting with the first step, left side. First step, the fittings just above the word "Bat" in both the picture and the drawing, it is a 1-inch 90° elbow, facing up. The second step is an 8-inch pipe connected to a 1-inch 90° elbow or ell, facing down with the top view. Then proceed until the complete base is connected, including the TOP VIEW BASE, which is inside the foundation, for it will be lifted to support the hanging ball (Step #4, which is the last step in construction).

838. *What is the third step in construction?*

Look at Step #2. This is a picture of the back side of the apparatus. Now, you have to construct the poles next. To get the length of the two rear poles (not including the fittings), count from the bottom of the left side, and you have: 12 inches, 12 inches, 21 inches, 13 inches, and 10 inches of pipe lengths, plus 11 inches of pipe length at the top of the apparatus. Take the 12 inches of pipe length, connect and turn the second 1-inch tee to the side, away from you, as shown in the drawing. Another 12-inch pipe length connected to the tee, facing you. Then a 21-inch pipe connected to a 1-inch tee, and proceed up to the top of the pole where you have a 1-inch elbow or ell, facing you. When the sections of the pole are together, put them in the fittings of the foundation of the apparatus (Step #2). The back poles of the apparatus are the tallest poles (back section of apparatus). Now, for the front poles (right side of drawing), you have a 1-inch ell, which is part of the foundation, at the bottom of the page. Then a 12-inch pipe length, 1-inch elbow at the top of the pole. These poles are inserted in the front part of the apparatus (Step #2). Now, you have a pole to the far right of the drawing. This pole is used for extra support for the hanging ball of the Bat Speed Apparatus, where the electric coated wire will go through for the adjustment of the ball.

839. *What is the fourth step in construction?*

The back and side supports (Step #3) hold up the four poles. Now, you might have to turn the fittings for the connection of the connecting bars. As for the left side, right side and the back side, you have bars which connect the poles. In connecting the bars, you can start from the bottom of the apparatus and work up. For example, first from the bottom is a 53-inch pipe length connected to one side of the pole, then the other side of the front and back pole. Connect another 53 inch pipe length for the other support for the front and back poles. Now, at the top of the connecting bars on the right side is a 1-inch cross, and on the left side is a 1-inch tee, which is used to support the TOP VIEW BASE. Then, all the cross support bars are in place (Step #3). Now, you have all the main supports to hold up all the sides.

840. What is the fifth step in construction?

Next (Step #4), connect the pipe lengths for the back support, then you pick up the TOP VIEW BASE, and put it into the fittings at the top, on each side of the apparatus.

841. How do you connect the swinging ball?

In the drawing, drill a hole in the hard ball or soft ball, push the wire through the ball, and tie a knot at the end so the ball does not fall out. Now, after threading the wire, as shown in the drawing, connect all fittings and pipes. Connect tarpaulins and you are finished for a lift time of enjoyment in the Art and Science of Baseball Practice.

BAT SPEED APPARATUS

THROWING PRACTICE   BAT SPEED PRACTICE

THROWING PLUS PRACTICE
WITH GROUND BALLS
AS IT RETURNS, OR FOR
THROWING USING THE
STEPPING SQUARE

HITTING PRACTICE:
1) BAT MASTER
2) TEE MASTER
3) STANCE AND
   STRIDE DEVICE

ASSEMBLE BAT-SPEED APPARATUS

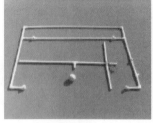

STEP #1
BASE

STEP #2
SIDES

STEP #3
BACKSIDES

STEP #4
TOP AND BACK

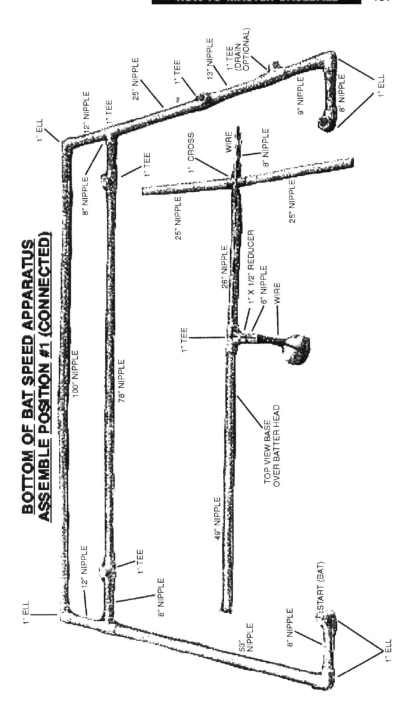

BOTTOM OF BAT SPEED APPARATUS
ASSEMBLE POSITION #1 (CONNECTED)

1" ELL
12" NIPPLE
1" TEE
25" NIPPLE
1" TEE
13" NIPPLE
1" TEE (DRAIN OPTIONAL)
9" NIPPLE
8" NIPPLE
1" ELL
1" ELL
8" NIPPLE
1" TEE
1" CROSS
WIRE
8" NIPPLE
25" NIPPLE
25" NIPPLE
26" NIPPLE
100" NIPPLE
78" NIPPLE
1" TEE
1" X 1/2" REDUCER
6" NIPPLE
WIRE
49" NIPPLE
TOP VIEW BASE OVER BATTER HEAD
12" NIPPLE
1" TEE
8" NIPPLE
53" NIPPLE
8" NIPPLE
START (BAT)
1" ELL
1" ELL

ASSEMBLE BAT-SPEED APPARATUS
ASSEMBLE POSITION #2

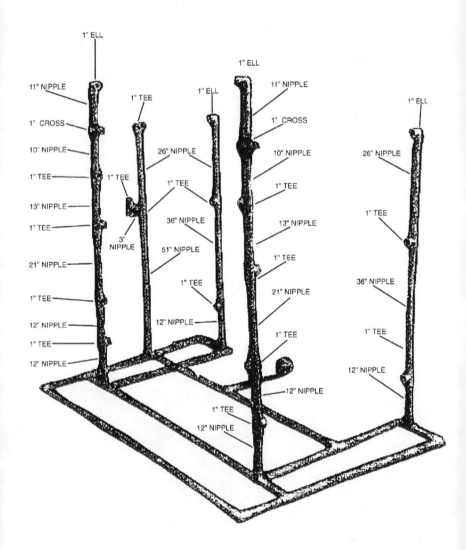

ASSEMBLE BAT-SPEED APPARATUS
ASSEMBLE POSITION #3

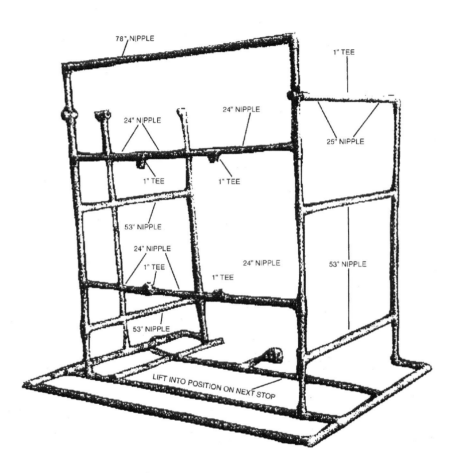

ASSEMBLE BAT-SPEED APPARATUS
ASSEMBLE POSITION #4

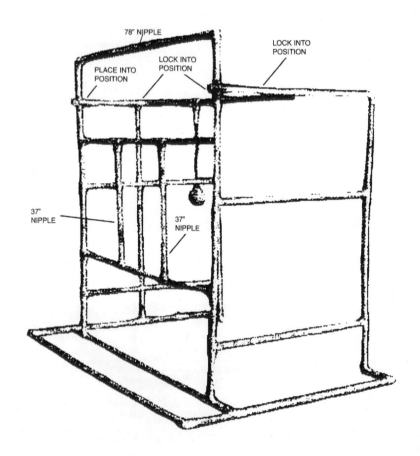

BAT-SPEED APPARATUS
FULLY ASSEMBLED

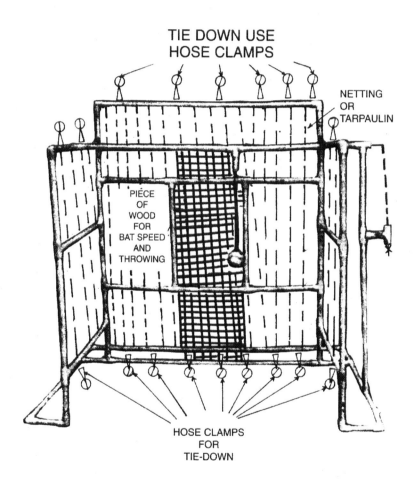

TIE DOWN USE
HOSE CLAMPS

NETTING
OR
TARPAULIN

PIECE
OF
WOOD
FOR
BAT SPEED
AND
THROWING

HOSE CLAMPS
FOR
TIE-DOWN

BACKSTOP MASTER

842. *Do you feel the Backstop Master is easy for portability?*

It depends on many things. How long the batter is going to practice? What kind of car does he/she drive? How many players do you have? In our opinion, we feel, if you are using the full size backstop, it will be a little difficult to transport. But if you cut the size in half, then it should not be too awkward.

843. *Can I make the Backstop Master smaller?*

Yes. When throwing, it should be about 6 feet wide instead of 10 feet wide. You can adjust the width to any size you think is necessary, but with hitting we suggest using the full size to start.

844. *Will I need the netting when using the Backstop Master for throwing?*

No, the netting is used for hitting only to reduce the speed of the hit ball. If the batter stands farther away from the Backstop Master, there is no need for netting. Also, the player can use a lighter backing than the canvas.

845. *How does a person construct the Backstop Master?*

First, you want to cut out the sizes for the base and lay it down as shown in the picture. Second, cut out the various sizes for the side sections. Now, do as in Step #1, connect all fittings and pipes. Then, as in Step #2, put up the sides. Third, put the top section together as in Step #3. Fourth, follow Step #4 and tie the canvas. Then, get some netting and place it in front of the canvas. Set up the Bat Master as shown in the picture or in Step #4.

BACKSTOP MASTER FOR PLAYING BASEBALL OR PRACTICE WITH BAT MASTER

BACKSTOP MASTER JR.
PRACTICE WITH TEE MASTER AND
STANCE AND STRIDE DEVICE
IN SMALL AREA OR
TEE MASTER AND HOME BASE

BACKSTOP MASTER
UNCONNECTED

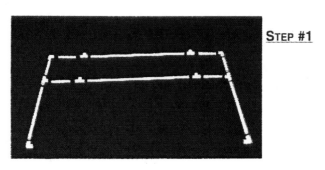

STEP #1

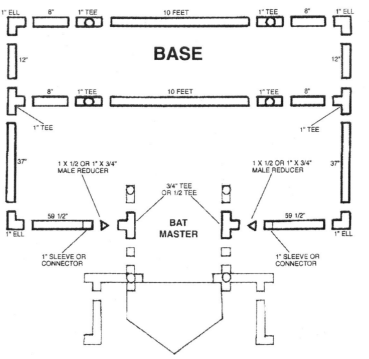

| 1" ELL | 8" | 1" TEE | 10 FEET | 1" TEE | 8" | 1" ELL |

BASE

12"   12"

| 8" | 1" TEE | 10 FEET | 1" TEE | 8" |

1" TEE   1" TEE

37"   37"

1 X 1/2 OR 1" X 3/4"
MALE REDUCER

3/4" TEE
OR 1/2 TEE

1 X 1/2 OR 1" X 3/4"
MALE REDUCER

59 1/2"   **BAT**
MASTER   59 1/2"

1" ELL   1" ELL

1" SLEEVE OR
CONNECTOR

1" SLEEVE OR
CONNECTOR

STEPS #1 AND #4

BACKSTOP MASTER
UNCONNECTED

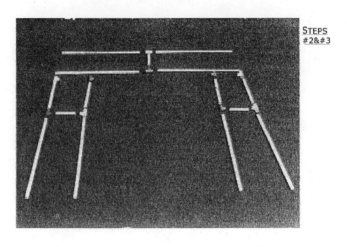

STEPS #2&#3

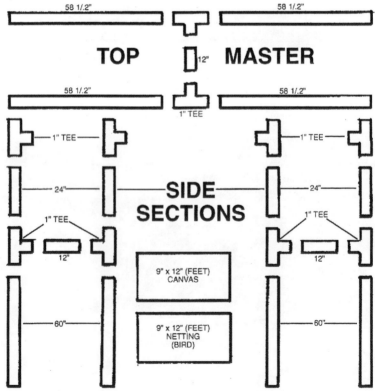

58 1/.2"   58 1/.2"

TOP   12"   MASTER

58 1/.2"   58 1/.2"

1" TEE

1" TEE   1" TEE   1" TEE   1" TEE

24"   **SIDE** **SECTIONS**   24"

1" TEE   1" TEE

12"   12"

9" x 12" (FEET) CANVAS

60"   9" x 12" (FEET) NETTING (BIRD)   60"

CONSTRUCT BACKSTOP MASTER WITH BAT MASTER CONNECTED

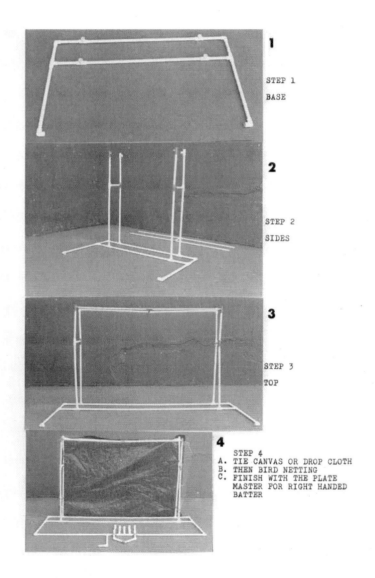

1

STEP 1

BASE

2

STEP 2

SIDES

3

STEP 3

TOP

4   STEP 4
A. TIE CANVAS OR DROP CLOTH
B. THEN BIRD NETTING
C. FINISH WITH THE PLATE
   MASTER FOR RIGHT HANDED
   BATTER

CONSTRUCT BASE OF BACKSTOP MASTER JR.

UNCONNECTED

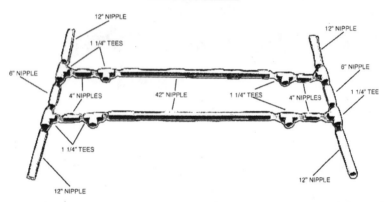

CONNECTED

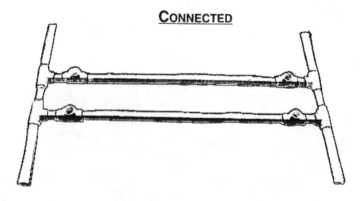

CONSTRUCT SIDES OF BACKSTOP MASTER JR.

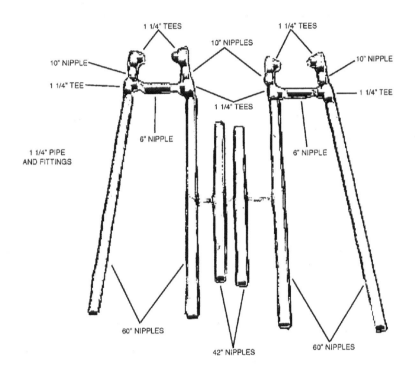

Top, Sides and Base of Backstop Master Jr.

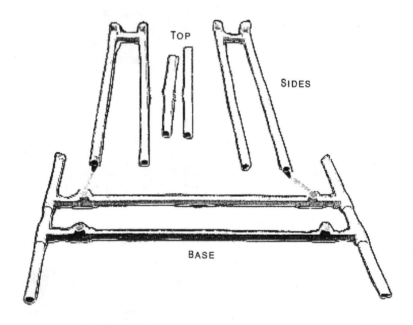

STEPPING SQUARE

846. *What is the Stepping Square?*

It is a device to help the player throw the ball properly when playing baseball. The player cannot have improper foot movement when using the Stepping Square. When adjusted to the player's height, he/she must not step outside the square for the proper throw.

847. *Explain the pictures on the Stepping Square, Steps #1 through #4 (Question 360)*

Step #1 is the front view of the stance. The model has his feet in the stance position ready to throw. The arm is back and the ball level with his ear. In Step #2, the model has taken his stride and has not quite released the ball. In step #3, in a split second, the model has followed through and released the ball as shown in Step #4. After the final release of the ball, he makes sure to finish up square, so he will have the proper balance. Each of these pictures is finished within seconds of each other.

848. *What is the average height as shown in the drawing?*

The measurements are only a guideline. After throwing for a while, the player will know the correct adjustment for the Stepping Square.

849. *Can a friend and I play catch with each having our own Stepping Square?*

Yes. You can also play catch as a game with each one losing a point if he/she steps out of the square.

850. *What of the picture in Steps #1 and #2?*

He has taken the ball and has released it at the target for the properly thrown ball. Notice on the finish up he has not stepped out of the Stepping Square at anytime, so he is using the device properly.

851. What material is needed for the Stepping Square? (PVC Plastic Pipes)

First, you will use 1/2-inch pipes and the "thinnest gauge" of 3/4-inch pipes. Second, you will need two 1/2-inch 90° elbows. Now, in exchange for the 1/2-inch elbows, you can have two 3/4-inch 90° elbows, four 3/4-inch x 1/2-inch reducers. Third, use hand clamps to make it a stationary adjustment. Fourth, 4 lengths of 3/4-inch pipe "thin gauge," each cut to a 3-foot length. Fifth, 4 lengths of 1/2-inch pipe each cut to a 2-foot length.

852. *Do you suggest in place of the two 3/4-inch 90° elbows and reducer, all I will need is two 1/2-inch 90° elbows?*

Yes, you can exchange either one.

853. *Where do I put the reducers on the 3/4-inch pipe?*

As you will notice in the drawing, two reducers into each 90° elbow.

854. *What are the final steps of assembly for the Stepping Square?*

Place the two 1/2-inch 90° elbows or the two 3/4-inch 90° elbows with reducers in opposite corners. Then, put the 1/2-inch pipe into each of the reducers (if using reducers). Next, slip the 3/4-inch pipe over the 1/2-pipe. Then, connect the rest of the two 3/4-inch 90° elbows, so it's a square.

855. *What is the Stepping Square Deluxe?*

It is used the same way as the Stepping Square, except it has a ball keeper so the balls the player is throwing will not roll away while practicing. Excellent for use on cement.

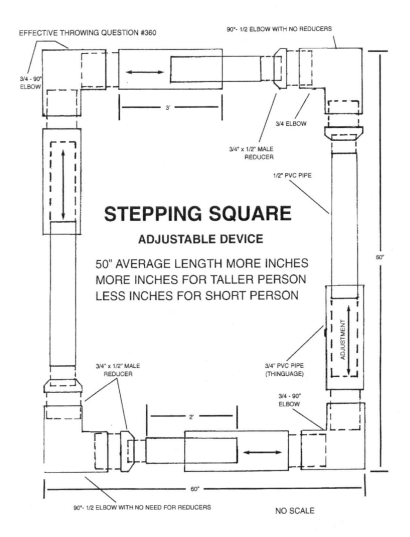

EFFECTIVE THROWING QUESTION #360

90°- 1/2 ELBOW WITH NO REDUCERS

3/4 - 90" ELBOW

3/4 ELBOW

3/4" x 1/2" MALE REDUCER

1/2" PVC PIPE

3'

STEPPING SQUARE

ADJUSTABLE DEVICE

50" AVERAGE LENGTH MORE INCHES
MORE INCHES FOR TALLER PERSON
LESS INCHES FOR SHORT PERSON

60"

ADJUSTMENT

3/4" x 1/2" MALE REDUCER

3/4" PVC PIPE (THINGUAGE)

3/4 - 90" ELBOW

2'

60"

90°- 1/2 ELBOW WITH NO NEED FOR REDUCERS

NO SCALE

Practice Throwing and Catching with Stepping Square Deluxe or Challenge Match for Master Thrower

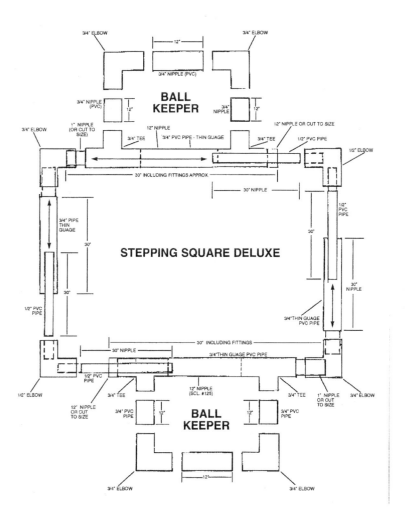

SUPER STRIKE MASTER 1 (SSM-1)

856. *What does the Super Strike Master 1 (SSM-1) represent?*
It performs like a base player with his/her arms fully extended in all directions with no movement, ready to catch a perfectly thrown ball.

857. *What is the purpose of the Super Strike Master 1 (SSM-1)?*
First, the SSM-1 helps the player throw the ball properly to other base positions on the infield. Second, it helps other base players practice throwing. Third, it helps outfielders practice throwing to the various base positions and home plate. Fourth, it helps the player visualize the correct throw. The more a player practices, the stronger the picture and the more accurate the throw.

858. *Why is the Super Strike Master (SSM-1) so important for a base player or outfielder when throwing?*
If the base player is trying out for a certain position, he/she needs to practice. Through necessity, some players can only practice alone. Without the SSM-1, the player cannot practice throwing properly, since he/she has no image of the player at the base. Place the SSM-1 at the base and it's as if a player was there catching the thrown balls. The thrower must have this surrogate player at the base in order to improve. The best invention that can provide the likeness is the Super Strike Master 1 (SSM-1).

859. *What if the thrower hits the center of the SSM-1 all the time?*
The coach must judge the player on how well he/she gets that throw to the other base player. If the player throws in

the center of the SSM-1 all the time, and if no other player can, then he/she should be the best thrower. The objective is not to have the base player moving in all directions or jumping when the ball is thrown. All the base player should have to do is to just catch the ball without displacement. This is accomplished when the SSM-1 is catching the ball in the center.

860. *While throwing, I hit the backstop of the SSM-1. Will that be a good throw?*

Yes. The SSM-1 is taking the place of the base player. If the ball hits the backstop, it means that it is within reach of the base player so he/she can catch the ball without getting off the base for the out. This is a good throw. If the ball hits the center of the SSM-I, it is an excellent throw.

861. *Can the size of the SSM-1 be adjusted for the different heights of the players?*

Yes, but only to a certain extent. If the players are small, measure from the knees to the shoulders, and reduce the support poles to that size. The base and top portions should not be changed. They are inter changeable with the Super Strike Master 2 (SSM-2). Remember, the measurements are fixed, so take the *shortest* player on the team and use those measurements.

862. *What about the arm reach?*

First, measure from the neck to the end of the wrist. Second, take the approximate length of the arm and reduce the arm support pipes to that length. Third, *do not make the SSM-1 any larger in size.*

863. *What about the catcher throwing to second base (picture)?*

Place the SSM-1 at second base, and place the catcher at home plate. The catcher should be about 127 feet away from the SSM-1, and should have about a dozen balls to throw at second base. Now, with the instructions on "How to Play Catcher" and with the SSM-1, the catcher can improve on the throw to second base with unlimited potential. The catcher can put the SSM-1 as low as possible and simulate the second base player tagging the base runner with the thrown ball.

864. *Why is the catcher's throw to second base so important?*

If the offensive team has a runner on first base, the base runner is going to try to steal second base. The catcher must have a good throwing arm to get that base runner out. For example, if the batter bunts the ball very close to the home base, the catcher will have time to make that long throw to second base (if the hit-and-run was not used). If the catcher can make that long throw to second base with accuracy and speed, then the base runner will be out and the second base player can try for a double play. *This type of play requires extensive practice.*

865. *I play third base. Will the SSM-1 benefit my throwing?*

Yes. First read the chapter on "How To Play Third Base." Second, place the SSM-1 at first base or about 127 feet away. Then start throwing. Remember, it takes time to improve. If the player misses the SSM-1, just keep on practicing. If the player is still having trouble, he/she should read the chapter on "Throwing Properly." The thrower can also use the "Stepping Square" for a real challenge in throwing scientifically.

866. *Why can't I use the Super Strike Master 2 as a base player?*

The SSM-1 is used as a base player and for throwing practice. It is more portable and about half the height and weight of the SSM-2. Each section had its own purpose. One person can move Section I by himself/herself. There are no adjustments to be made on Section I; all the parts are stationary.

867. *Is there some type of padding that goes around the steel pipe of the Super Strike Master 1?*

Yes, use pipe insulation foam. If the thrower is fast and the ball hits the front of the SSM-1, it will cut the leather around the baseball after a short period of time. The pipe insulation foam should only go around the front of the device where the ball might hit in order to protect it upon impact. The thrower should use old baseballs.

868. *What about steps for construction?*

Remember, follow each step closely. Take your time, starting with the support base and building upward. It took years to develop this device, so take your time and you should be well pleased with it, as we are. Good luck!

869. *On the Top and Bottom Sections, why on one picture does it show 8 inches and 7-1/2 inches on the other picture?*

I am showing you two different sizes because if the Hardware Store does not have the 7-1/2-inch nipples, then buy the 8-inch nipples, both will work fine. Just make sure you pick one or the other. Do not mix the 7-1/2-inch with the 8-inch nipples.

PRACTICE THROWING WITH *SSM1* TO HOME BASE
AND USE STEPPING SQUARE, CHALLENGE MATCH,
THROW TO VARIOUS BASES FOR MASTER BASE POSITIONS:
MASTER FIRST BASE, MASTER SHORTSTOP,
MASTER THIRD BASE ETC.

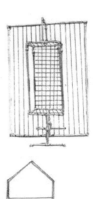

*PRACTICE THROWING WITH SSM1 TO SECOND
BASE OR CHALLENGE MATCH FOR MASTER
CATCHER, THROWING TO VARIOUS BASES*

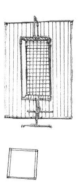

ASSEMBLE TOP SECTION OF SSM1
START AT BASE AND WORK UP FOR ASSEMBLY

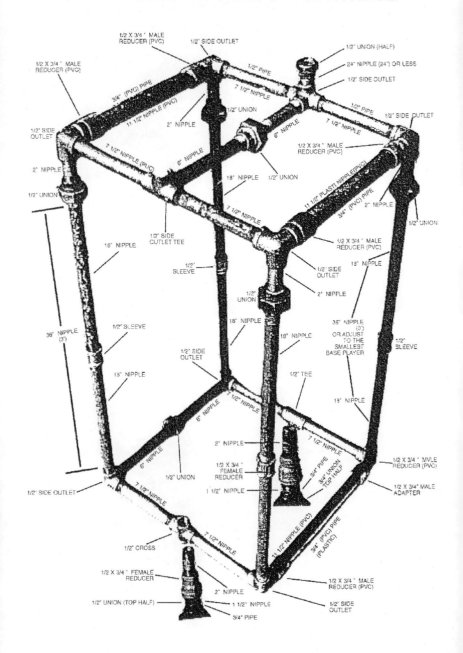

ASSEMBLE *SSM1* WITH *PADDED FRONT*

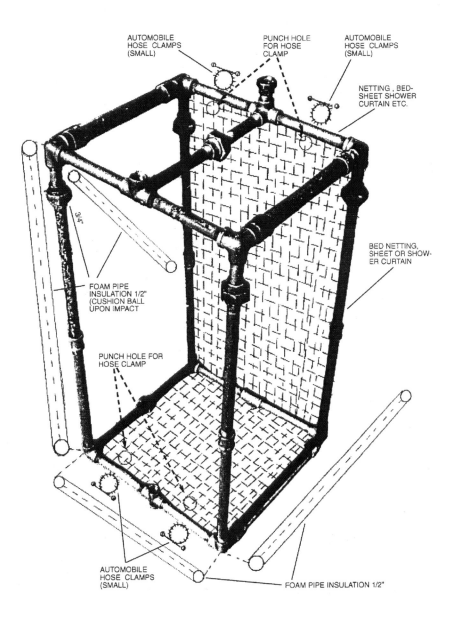

AUTOMOBILE HOSE CLAMPS (SMALL)

PUNCH HOLE FOR HOSE CLAMP

AUTOMOBILE HOSE CLAMPS (SMALL)

NETTING , BED-SHEET SHOWER CURTAIN ETC.

3/4"

FOAM PIPE INSULATION 1/2" (CUSHION BALL UPON IMPACT

BED NETTING, SHEET OR SHOW-ER CURTAIN

PUNCH HOLE FOR HOSE CLAMP

AUTOMOBILE HOSE CLAMPS (SMALL)

FOAM PIPE INSULATION 1/2"

BASE FOR SSM1 AND SSM2
TOP, BOTTOM AND BASE ARE INTERCHANGEABLE
WITH SSM2
CONNECTED

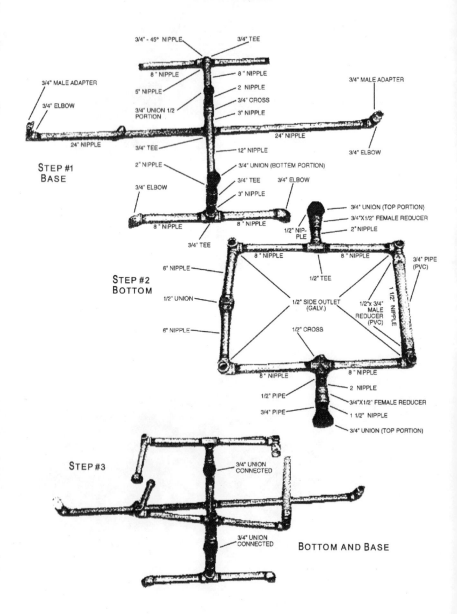

STEP #1
BASE

3/4" - 45° NIPPLE
3/4" TEE
8 " NIPPLE
8 " NIPPLE
3/4" MALE ADAPTER
5" NIPPLE
2 NIPPLE
3/4" MALE ADAPTER
3/4" ELBOW
3/4" CROSS
3/4" UNION 1/2 PORTION
3" NIPPLE
3/4" ELBOW
24" NIPPLE
24" NIPPLE
3/4" TEE
12" NIPPLE
3/4" ELBOW
2" NIPPLE
3/4" UNION (BOTTOM PORTION)
3/4" ELBOW
3/4" TEE
3/4" ELBOW
3" NIPPLE
8 " NIPPLE
8 " NIPPLE
3/4" TEE

STEP #2
BOTTOM

3/4" UNION (TOP PORTION)
3/4"X1/2" FEMALE REDUCER
2" NIPPLE
1/2" NIP-PLE
8 " NIPPLE
8 " NIPPLE
3/4" PIPE (PVC)
6" NIPPLE
1/2" TEE
1 1/2" NIPPLE
1/2" UNION
1/2" SIDE OUTLET (GALV.)
1/2"x 3/4" MALE REDUCER (PVC)
6" NIPPLE
1/2" CROSS
8 " NIPPLE
8 " NIPPLE
1/2" PIPE
2 NIPPLE
3/4"X1/2" FEMALE REDUCER
3/4" PIPE
1 1/2" NIPPLE
3/4" UNION (TOP PORTION)

STEP #3

3/4" UNION CONNECTED

BOTTOM AND BASE

3/4" UNION CONNECTED

Assemble Base, Top, Side (SSM1)

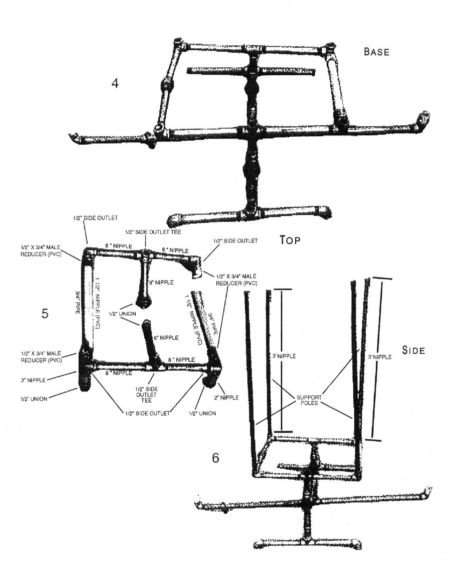

Super Strike Master1 (SSM1)
Top Ball Stopper

Step #7   **Connected**

SUPER STRIKE MASTER
SECTION 1
STEPS FOR CONSTRUCTION

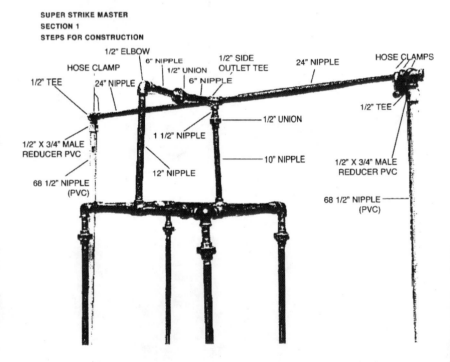

SUPER STRIKE MASTER
SECTION 1
MAINLY USED FOR BASE AND
OUTFIELD THROWING PRACTICE

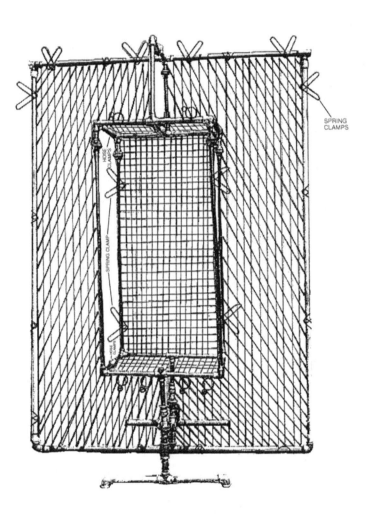

SUPER STRIKE MASTER 2 (SSM-2)

870. *What is the Super Strike Master 2 (SSM-2)?*

First, it is a device to help the player throw the ball properly in the strike zone of the batter. Second, it lets the batter get proper hitting so he/she will know what his/her own personal strike zone looks like while the pitched ball is in flight. Third, it can be adjusted to any batter for the proper strike zone. Finally, it can be used as a catcher, umpire, backstop, and batting cage.

871. *Is the Super Strike Master 2 very portable?*

The SSM-2 is not very portable. It takes at least two persons to move it unless it is taken apart. The one purpose of this component is for hitting, so the batter knows his/her strike zone with precise accuracy.

872. *What's so important about the SSM-2 being a portable batting backstop?*

Have you ever gone to a park and seen how many batting backstops there are? Sometimes one or two, but no more than that; the rest is wasted, nonproductive park. Now with the SSM-2, the player or players can get a small part of the park and make his/her own baseball diamond (no catcher is necessary).

873. *What about the different sections of the SSM-1 and SSM-2?*

Each section is detachable from the base for quick change, from one section to the other. The player can go from base throwing to hitting by changing the sections in a matter of minutes.

874. Does the player need two complete separate sections?

No. If the player has made the SSM-1 and wants to save money, all he/she will need are the adjustment pipes, the dividers, and Section 1 or 2. The player keeps the top and bottom portions. Then the player need only change the length of the adjustment pipes of each section and attach the dividers. It will take a little longer going form one component to the other, but you will save some money. Remember, this is a lifetime apparatus and if the player has the extra money, it is well worth having two separate sections. If the player has only one section, as time passes, the pipe will rust and the person will need some tools and oil to take them apart. If the steel pipes remain outside over a longer period of time, we suggest you paint them to control rust.

875. Can I use the Super Strike Master 2 in Slow-Pitch Baseball?

No. The ball does not travel on a horizontal plane. The slow pitch has a larger arc when thrown. If the ball travels on a horizontal plane as in Fast Pitch Underhand Baseball, however, then the SSM-2 will work very well.

876. Can the SSM-2 be used as a backstop while hitting (no catcher)?

Yes. With the Foul Ball Blocker attachment and the backstop, it can be used as a hitting apparatus. When the player puts the Foul Ball Blocker to the Backstop, the player has a portable batting cage.

877. What is the Foul Ball Blocker of the SSM-2?

It blocks foul balls as they are hit by the batter, whether he/she is a left-handed batter or a right-handed batter.

878. Will the backstop block most balls?

Yes, if the ball is misthrown or if the foul ball is hit low enough, the Foul Ball Blocker will block the balls. When using my method in hitting, the balls will not be going in all directions. The batter will have very few foul balls.

879. How can the SSM-2 be an umpire?

Throw the ball inside the SSM-2 (after being adjusted to the batter) for a strike. Use the Separator and it can call the pitches better than an umpire. If the ball is caught in the SSM-2 it is a strike. There is no argument about whether it is inside, outside, or a high or low pitch.

880. *What is the Removable Separator?*

It is a removable part of the SSM-2. It divides the strike zone into separate portions so the thrower can see what he/she needs to practice on. The Separator displays the high inside corner, high outside corner, middle ball inside, and so on. It shows every pitch the thrower needs to practice on in the strike zone, whether he/she is a left-handed or right-handed batter.

881. *What are the Removable Isolators?*

They are part of the Separator. They divide the strike zone into portions, so the thrower can pitch any type of ball.

882. *What are the Dividers on the Super Strike Master 2 and the Super Strike Master Jr.?*

The Dividers are what mark the separate areas of the strike zone of the batter. The Separator serves the same purpose. The difference is that the Dividers move up and down the adjustment pipes, so that each portion of the strike zone can be adjusted to each batter in a matter of seconds. The Separator is stationary and not quite as accurate as the Dividers, but they both serve the same purpose. The Dividers control the movement of the netting so the ball can be caught. Its main design is for high and low pitches. To have separate sections, like the Separator, the player needs a Bungee Cord down the middle to separate the different portions for various pitches.

883. *As the thrower, if I throw all strikes, how does the Separator help me?*

A. If the thrower can throw all strikes with the SSM-2 or Super Strike Master Jr. (discussed later in the chapter), then he/she needs to sharpen his/her throwing even more, so the thrower is sure of the pitches. With the Separator, the thrower gets a more accurate picture in his/her mind of the pitch he/she is throwing. It is excellent for the coach to pick out the pitchers. If the coach says, "Throw the high inside ball, left-handed batter," then the pitcher should try and throw the high inside ball. The best pitcher is the one who can do it consistently or as many times as necessary to that specific area of the strike zone.

884. *As a pitcher, can I challenge another pitcher to decide who is better?*

Yes, we would think so. Now, for the first time, two pitchers can challenge each other to see which one is the more accurate thrower (no catcher for this test). Without the SSM-2 or Super Strike Master Jr., the pitchers would not know for certain who is more accurate.

885. *Which player will use the Separator the most?*

The Separator is the most essential apparatus for the pitcher. For players who want to be pitchers on the team, the Separator will help them learn to throw with precision.

886. *How should the thrower or pitcher use the Separator?*

First, use the SSM-2 without the Separator (this also refers to the Super Strike Master Jr.). When the thrower can throw strike balls consistently, then he/she needs more of a challenge in throwing. Second, use the center of the Separator (any portions of the Separator are Isolators), which splits the strike zone in half. Now, the thrower thinks to him/herself, "Outside ball, right-handed batter." The thrower is to throw to the outside portion of the Isolator for a right-handed batter (ID #12). When the thrower can do that at any given time, the thrower is to move to another stage of throwing by using the Separator with all its Isolators. Third, when starting out, the thrower should pick the strongest pitch first, such as the middle ball, waist-high, left—or right-handed batter (ID #21 or #22). Then move to the more difficult types of pitches. For instance, the low-outside corner pitches (ID #23 and #24); then the high pitch inside (ID #35 and #36). Now, when the coach says, "Low outside ball, left-handed batter (ID #24)," the pitcher can throw this with no difficulty. Remember, all this takes time and practice. The thrower should decide just how good he/she wishes to be.

887. *I don't know if I am good enough to be a pitcher on the team. Will the SSM-2 and the Separator help me?*

Most definitely, yes. The player can practice alone and decide for him/herself whether to become a pitcher. Each player on the team has the potential to be a pitcher, but sometimes other players are not available to practice with. When practicing alone, a player can make mistakes and not feel embarrassed. Players have no excuse for not playing baseball, when they have their own private player—the Super Strike Master 2 and the Separator. Also, SSM1 for base player.

888. *Can the thrower use the Separator in Fast Pitch Softball?*

Yes. The player can use the SSM-2 or Super Strike Master Jr. with any type of baseball where the ball travels on a horizontal plane. Since the ball is larger in softball than hardball, we would suggest the softball thrower use the Bungee Cords (elastic stretch cords) at all times when practicing throwing. The thrower can utilize the Bungee Cords in place of the Separator (note picture).

889. *What is the purpose of the Bungee Cords when using the SSM-2?*

Bungee Cords are used for when the thrower has a batter at the plate. They enable the thrower to see where the various pitches go, as well as tell the batter what each pitch look like as it approaches. With this method of using the SSM-2, the player can prove even further that my method of hitting is correct. For example, if the batter over strides and drops his/her shoulder, the thrower should pitch the fast ball, inside-high, and the batter will be lucky to hit a foul ball. Read the chapter, "How to be a Pitcher." Thus, the thrower will know what to pitch to each batter with specific perfection so as to handicap the batter in hitting.

890. *Why can't the thrower use the Separator when there is a batter hitting?*

Remember, the ball will bounce off the steel pipe and might hit the batter. Use the Bungee Cords whenever there is a batter at the plate.

891. *What is a good game for two players using the SSM-2?*

As with all games, use your imagination. First, get twelve hard balls, or whatever the players want to use in the game, such as semi-hard or semi-soft ball, Second, one player throws while the other hits. Third, throw three-quarter style (no sidearm throwing) as instructed in the book.

Fourth, the batter is allowed one or two strikes (depending on what level you are at). Fifth, the pitcher chases all balls hit by the batter. Sixth, the pitcher goes to bat. Seventh, play as many innings as you like until one person quits or you both decide the game is tied. Eight, all games are fun. Do not get upset if you lose. Just go out and have a good time. Also, play penalty player to keep it a challenge, such as letting the batter have three strikes instead of two. This allows for extra practice in hitting and throwing.

892. *Can we use the same game as a challenge match?*

Yes, but the rules will be a little different. Now, this can decide who the better hitters and throwers are on the team. This makes the old saying, "Pitchers can't hit," a misleading statement. For now, the pitcher will have to hit as well as pitch.

893. *If I play the outfield and challenge the shortstop for his/her position, should I have that position if I win the challenge match?*

Yes, but can the outfielder make that long throw to first base with the same accuracy as the shortstop? This is another test. The SSM-2 puts a whole new perspective on baseball. If you are the best player on the team, you should have the choice of any position on the team because you can throw and hit better than anyone else.

894. *Will this method take the place of the coach?*

No, but it should assist coaches in making their conclusions. Coaches can use this as a test in forming their decision. When players have the proper attitude they will know what position to play. When players have unpleasant attitudes, get into lawlessness, and do not get along with other players, perhaps they should not be on the team, even if the player should be number one in the challenge match. The first concern is for the team. The team must have unity and harmony in order to win. It is up to the best players on the team to establish an example for other players—by staying out of trouble and keeping grades up in school.

895. *Who has the final declaration on all positions?*

The coach has the final word in deciding which position each team member will play. If the player feels he/she is being treated unfairly for some reason, then a third person should be involved. But this should be a last resort. The player should try to talk to the coach before going to a third party. If the coach is very stubborn, maybe the coach should look to a third person for advice. This is not a matter of who the boss is, but a concern for what is good for the player, as well as for the team. Again, the coach's authority should be respected here.

896. *What would be some of the rules for a challenge match using the SSM-2?*

These rules may vary, but once decided they must be adhered to throughout the baseball season. The coach and players should work together on the rules to make them fair, so that there is no argument as to what is suitable. The following will serve as a guide:

Rule 1:   Twelve baseballs to start throwing.

Rule 2:   Two foul balls equal one strike. Two strikes equal one out. Three balls equal a base hit. Two outs per inning.

Rule 3:   Have a home run and infield, and mark off the distance and use a string, flour or shirt for the marks.

Rule 4:   No penalty player; both have same rules.

Rule 5:   Play seven or nine innings or until one player quits.

Rule 6:   Batter chases his/her own foul balls after the inning.

Rule 7:   Once the pitcher winds up, the batter cannot step out of the batter's box. It will be a strike if the ball is thrown.

Rule 8:   If a ground ball goes to the pitcher and he/she catches it, that will be an out. If the ball stops before this pitcher can pick it up, this will be a strike.

Rule 9:   If a ground ball passes the pitcher, it will be a base hit. If a ground ball passes the pitcher and stops, it will be a base hit.

Rule 10:   If a ground ball or fly ball is dropped by pitcher, it will be a base hit.

Rule 11: If a fly ball or line drive is not caught by the pitcher, but goes past the infield, it will be a double base hit.

Rule 12: Referee calls each hit and home run as game is played. At end of inning, the score is told to both players and they will agree on the score.

Rule 13: After the inning, the pitcher will pick up all balls (except foul balls) and prepare to bat within ten minutes. Otherwise, this constitutes a delay of game and a penalty will be charged.

Rule 14: If pitcher is out of balls, he/she has ten minutes to pick up balls and start throwing. Otherwise, a delay of game is charged. Two delays will forfeit the match. If one delay takes longer than fifteen minutes, the pitcher defaults the match.

Rule 15: Allow ten minutes rest between innings, including the time to pick up balls. One delay of game loses one home run. Two delays will default the match. *Apply to both batter and pitcher.*

Rule 16: In an argument, the referee has the final ruling.

Rule 17: First time batter hits with thrown ball, pitcher loses home run. Second time, the pitcher will forfeit the tournament, as well as possible suspension for a certain period of time (not too severe on this rule if accidental). Thus, referee should notice if the pitcher is apologetic about hitting the batter. Note: Some players walk in front of the ball to win the tournament. BE CAREFUL ON THIS RULING (does not apply to slow pitch).

Rule 18: If the batter throws a bat out of anger, it will be an out. If this is done three times the batter will default the match.

Rule 19: Any player who assaultively touches another player will be suspended and sit out the next game, depending on the harm done to the other player. If a player causes another to be hurt, the offender should not be able to play for the whole season.

Rule 20:   At the end of the tournament both players must shake hands and say, "Thank you," using the other player's first name, such as "Thank you, Bill," or "Thank you, Sue." Otherwise, a player will be suspended. Referee will give two warnings on this matter.

897.   *Should the player specialize in one position?*

No. This is not football where size and strength make the difference. It is not basketball where height and ball handing technique makes the difference. Size and speed do not make much difference when there is no body contact. After reading my book, the player will know the positions and how to play them well. We tell the player to move around to various positions to be able to play them all, but players should have a favorite position.

898.   *I can't beat any of the players on the team. What can I do?*

Ask the coach. There are only two answers for that question, in my opinion. First, read the book, devise the teaching tools. Second, practice, practice. The player who practices the most, participates on the team. This is a way for the team to say, "These are the best players the school or club has; try to defeat us." Players must practice to make the team. This is the only fair way. Players should earn their positions on the team. That is why we like the inventions so much; they give every player an equal chance.

899.   *What can I do if I still don't make the team?*

Ask the coach if you can start up another team. Call this team the "U" team or the "Underdogs." Then challenge the "A" team for fun. Nothing is more exciting than to see the "Underdogs" beat the best team. *Be ready for comments, coach, if the "A" team loses.*

PRACTICE THROWING AND HITTING WITH *SSM2*
CHALLENGE MATCH FOR MASTER HITTER AND
MASTER THROWER
NO CATCHER REQUIRED

BUNGEE CORDS   NO BUNGEE CORDS

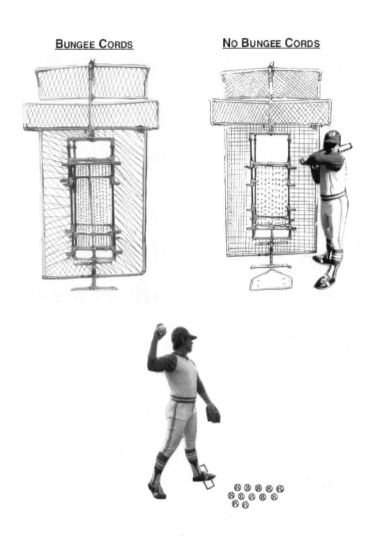

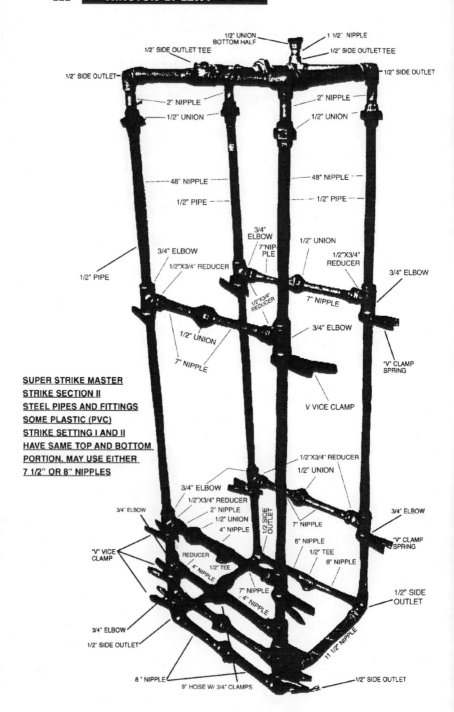

SUPER STRIKE MASTER
STRIKE SECTION II
STEEL PIPES AND FITTINGS
SOME PLASTIC (PVC)
STRIKE SETTING I AND II
HAVE SAME TOP AND BOTTOM
PORTION, MAY USE EITHER
7 1/2" OR 8" NIPPLES

Center Section of SSM2

SUPER STRIKE MASTER
STRIKE SECTION II
STEEL PIPES AND FITTINGS
SOME PLASTIC (PVC)

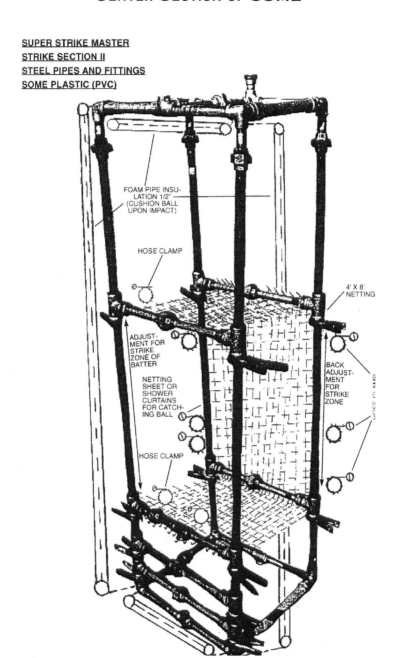

FOAM PIPE INSU-
LATION 1/2" —
(CUSHION BALL
UPON IMPACT)

HOSE CLAMP

4' X 8'
NETTING

ADJUST-
MENT FOR
STRIKE
ZONE OF
BATTER

NETTING
SHEET OR
SHOWER
CURTAINS
FOR CATCH-
ING BALL

BACK
ADJUST-
MENT
FOR
STRIKE
ZONE

HOSE CLAMP

HOSE CLAMP

SSM2 WITHOUT SUPPORT POLES

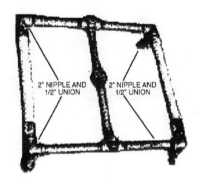

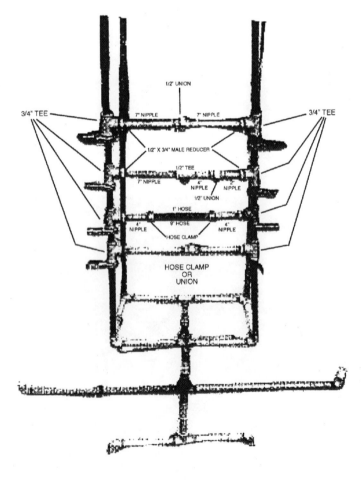

INTERCHANGEABLE BASE WITH SSM2
SIDES AND SUPPORT SSM2
ASSEMBLY CONTINUES FROM SSM1

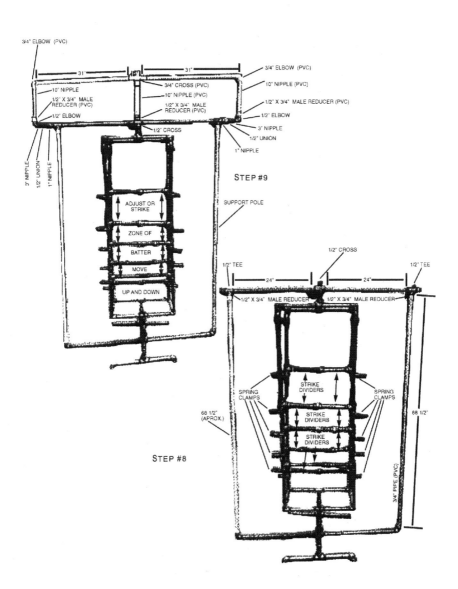

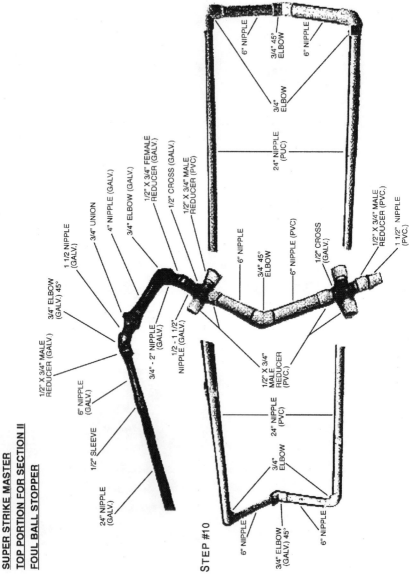

SUPER STRIKE MASTER
TOP PORTION FOR SECTION II
FOUL BALL STOPPER

STEP #10

1/2" X 3/4" MALE REDUCER (GALV.)

6" NIPPLE (GALV.)

1/2" SLEEVE

24" NIPPLE (GALV.)

3/4" ELBOW (GALV.) 45°

1 1/2 NIPPLE (GALV.)

3/4" UNION

4" NIPPLE (GALV.)

3/4" ELBOW (GALV.)

1/2" X 3/4" FEMALE REDUCER (GALV.)

1/2" CROSS (GALV.)

1/2" X 3/4" MALE REDUCER (PVC)

3/4" - 2" NIPPLE (GALV.)

1/2" - 1 1/2" NIPPLE (GALV.)

6" NIPPLE

3/4" 45° ELBOW

6" NIPPLE (PVC)

1/2" CROSS (GALV.)

1/2" X 3/4" MALE REDUCER (PVC.)

1 1/2" NIPPLE (PVC.)

1/2" X 3/4" MALE REDUCER (PVC.)

24" NIPPLE (PVC)

3/4" ELBOW

6" NIPPLE

3/4" ELBOW (GALV.) 45°

6" NIPPLE

6" NIPPLE

3/4" 45° ELBOW

6" NIPPLE

3/4" ELBOW

24" NIPPLE (PVC)

SUPER STRIKE MASTER
STRIKE SECTION II
PRACTICE HITTING AND THROWING

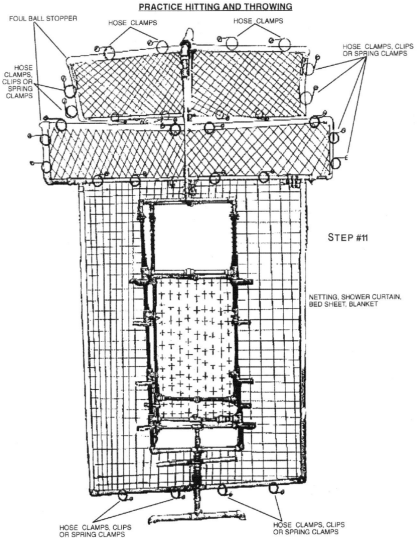

SSM2 VARIOUS SECTIONS OF SEPARATOR FOR PRACTICE THROWING *MASTER THROWERS ONLY

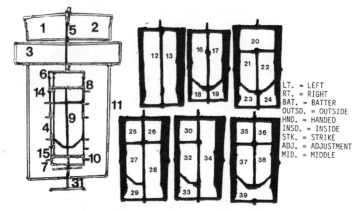

LT. = LEFT
RT. = RIGHT
BAT. = BATTER
OUTSD. = OUTSIDE
HND. = HANDED
INSD. = INSIDE
STK. = STRIKE
ADJ. = ADJUSTMENT
MID. = MIDDLE

STRIKE MASTER SHOWING STRIKE ZONE OF BATTER AND THE VARIOUS SECTIONS FOR DIFFERENT PITCHES FOR THE THROWER TO AIM AT.

1. STOPS FOUL BALLS FOR LT. HND. BAT.
2. STOPS FOUL BALLS FOR RT. HND. BAT.
3. OVERTHROWN BALLS NOT IN STK. ZONE.
4. SUPPORT POLES FOR SECTION II.
5. SUPPORT POLE FOR BALL STOPPERS.
6. INTERCHANGE FOR TOP SECTION I.
7. INTERCHANGE FOR BOTTOM SECTION I.
8. DIVIDER ADJ. FOR HIGH STRIKE ZONE.
9. SEPARATOR & STK. ZONE OF BAT.
10. SEPARATOR SUPPORT DIVIDER LOW STK. ZONE.
11. SUPPORT POLES.
12. OUTSD. STK. ZONE BALL FOR RT. HND. BAT. & INSD. STK. ZONE BALL FOR LT. HND. BAT.
13. INSD. STK. ZONE BALL FOR RT. HND. BAT. & OUTSD. STK. ZONE BALL FOR LT. HND. BAT.
14. BACK DIVIDER NET ADJ. FOR HIGH BALLS.
15. BACK DIVIDER NET ADJ. FOR LOW BALLS.
16. MID. & HIGH OUTSD. STK. ZONE FOR RT. HND BAT.
17. MID. & HIGH INSD. STK. ZONE FOR RT. HND. BAT. & MID. & HIGH OUTSD. STK. ZONE FOR LT. HND. BAT.
18. LOW OUTSD. STK. ZONE FOR RT. HND. BAT & LOW INSD. STK. ZONE FOR LT. HND. BAT.
19. LOW INSD. STK. ZONE FOR RT. HND. BAT. & LOW OUTSD. STK. ZONE FOR LT. HND. BAT.
20. HIGH STK. ZONE FOR LT. & RT. HND. BAT.
21. MID. OUTSD. STK. ZONE FOR RT. HND. BAT. & MID. INSD. STK. ZONE FOR LT. HND. BAT.
22. MID. INSD. STK. ZONE FOR RT. HND. BAT. AND MID. OUTSD. STK. ZONE LT. HND. BAT.
23. SAME AS #18.

24. SAME AS #19.
25. HIGH OUTSD. STK. ZONE FOR RT. HND. BAT. ALSO HIGH INSIDE STK. ZONE FOR LT. HND. BAT.
26. HIGH INSD. STK. ZONE FOR RT. HND. BAT. AND HIGH OUTSD. STK. ZONE FOR LT. HND. BAT.
27. SAME AS # 21.
28. MID. & LOW INSD. STK. ZONE FOR RT. HND. BAT. AND MID. & LOW OUTSD. STK. ZONE LT. HND. BAT.
29. SAME AS #18 & #23.
30. SAME AS #25.
31. BASE FOR BACKSTOP & TIE DOWN FOR NETTING.
32. SAME AS #21 & #27
33. SAME AS #18, #23 & #29
34. SAME AS #13
35. SAME AS #25 & #30
36. SAME AS #26
37. SAME AS #21, #27 & #32
38. SAME AS #22
39. LOW STK. ZONE FOR LT. AND RT. HND. BAT.

SUPER STRIKE MASTER JR.

900. *Can I hang netting over the back of the SSM-J to stop the ball?*

> That is correct. You can hang netting over the back of the SSM-J to stop the ball if thrown properly.

901. *Does the SSM-J need a backstop?*

> Yes and No. At the early stages of throwing, the player will understand that the SSM-J is the most advanced apparatus for the thrower. If he/she wants a backstop, the Backstop Master is the device for the player to use. We will admit the SSM-J is more portable, and if the player adds the Backstop Master, it will be very bulky and bothersome for one person to carry. Now, if the thrower has a catcher that does not want to recoup misthrown balls, then the Backstop Master is an essential tool. Let the thrower decide among the multitude of ways they want to use the SSM-J.

902. *Is the SSM-J very portable?*

> The SSM-J is very compact. The SSM-J, because it is so lightweight, is the best for throwing, hitting, and catching.

903. *Can I use the Separator with the SSM-J?*

> Yes. This is for the catcher as well. Use the cords as you did with the SSM-2, but now the thrower has a catcher to catch the ball, as well as a hitter. The thrower, hitter, and catcher can all get excellent practice.

904. *Can it help a person who wants to be a catcher for the first time?*

That is correct. You can hang netting over the back of the SSM-J to stop the ball if not thrown properly.

905. *What would be the steps for teaching a beginning catcher using the SSM-J?*

First, read the chapter on "How to be a Catcher." Second, place the catcher behind the SSM-J, then adjust the strike zone and throw the pitches. Third, use the Bungee Cord down the middle. Fourth, use all the Bungee Cords or Separator. Fifth, place a batter in front of the SSM-J with the Bungee Cords, but don't let the batter swing at the ball as it is thrown by the pitcher. Sixth, let the batter swing at the ball, but don't let the batter hit the ball. Seventh, now the catcher should be ready to play baseball. As each level is reached, the self-confidence of the catcher will develop tremendously. This is one of the characteristics the coach wants in a good catcher: To build up his/her assurance to catch that ball behind the plate. Remember, each sequential level requires time and practice.

906. *How does the SSM-J assist any catcher?*

When the catcher is catching the ball behind the plate, and when the batter swings the bat, the bat interferes with the catcher's vision of the ball as it approaches and the catcher will sometimes close his/her eyes at the last split second and drop the ball. Now, the SSM-J will eliminate that problem, as it simulates the batter in swinging at the ball (using Bungee Cords). Therefore, if the coach puts a batter up at home base with the SSM-J behind the hitter it will obstruct a certain amount of the catcher's vision even more when the batter swings at the ball in flight. So, the more the catcher's vision is temporarily interrupted during practice, the better he/she will play during a regular game, when the SSM-J is removed.

907. *Can the SSM-J be used the same way in underhand fast pitch with a softball?*

Yes. If it is Fast Pitch Underhand or Overhand, the SSM-J can be used superbly when throwing.

908. *Can I use the SSM-J in a challenge match?*

Yes. The person who picks up the most misthrown balls will lose the match.

909. *Can the SSM-J be used as a base player like the SSM-1?*

Yes, but the thrower must again be very accurate in throwing. When players want to put some pressure on themselves in base throwing, this device is extremely helpful. It is like penalizing yourself if you miss the perfect throw, for then the player will have to regain the ball.

910. *Is the SSM-J cheaper to construct than the SSM-1 or SSM-2?*

Yes. That is another advantage of the SSM-J; it is less expensive to build than the SSM-1 or SSM-2. So the player can take that into account when choosing.

911. *Why the different pedestals on the SSM-J?*

The different bottoms are used strictly for balance on the SSM-J. The substructures give the player a choice between Base 1 (SSMJ), Base 2 (SSMJC) or Base 3 (Slide Master).

912. *Where can a person buy the parts for all your inventions?*

Any hardware store has the necessary components and if not available, they can be ordered. As for the netting, if the player does not like the sheet, blanket, or tarpaulin, then use the netting. I bought the netting at a surplus store.

Practice Throwing to Home Plate with Batter and Catcher (SSMJ) Use Bungee Cords Only, Not Separator Challenge Match for Master Hitter

SEPARATOR

BUNGEE CORDS

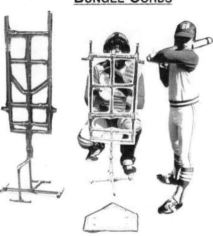

PRACTICE THROWING AND HITTING WITH SSMJ
OR THE SSMJC
NO CATCHER IS NECESSARY
PRACTICE THROWING ALONE
WITH SEPARATOR OR BUNGEE CORDS WITH BATTER
SEPARATOR FOR ADVANCED THROWING ONLY

ALSO USE THE STEPPING SQUARE

CHALLENGE MATCH FOR MASTER HITTER, MASTER
CATCHER, SUPERIOR MASTER THROWER OR
SUPERIOR MASTER BASE POSITION

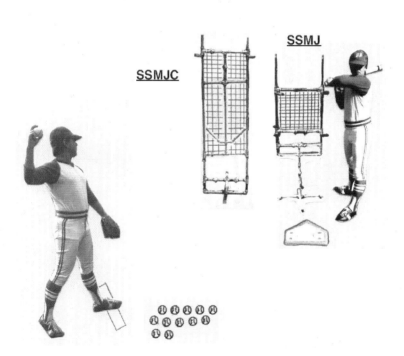

SSMJ

SSMJC

BASE FOR *SSMJ*

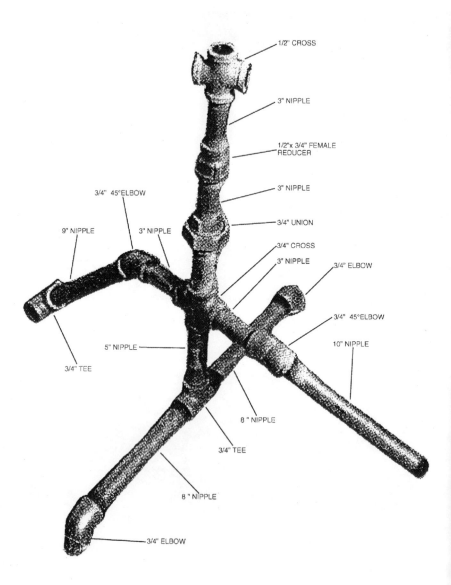

1/2" CROSS

3" NIPPLE

1/2"x 3/4" FEMALE REDUCER

3" NIPPLE

3/4" UNION

3/4" 45°ELBOW

9" NIPPLE

3" NIPPLE

3/4" CROSS

3" NIPPLE

3/4" ELBOW

3/4" 45°ELBOW

10" NIPPLE

5" NIPPLE

3/4" TEE

8 " NIPPLE

3/4" TEE

8 " NIPPLE

3/4" ELBOW

SUPPORT FOR SIDES OF SSMJ

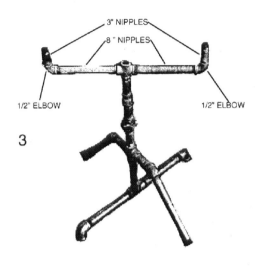

3" NIPPLES

8 " NIPPLES

1/2" ELBOW   1/2" ELBOW

3

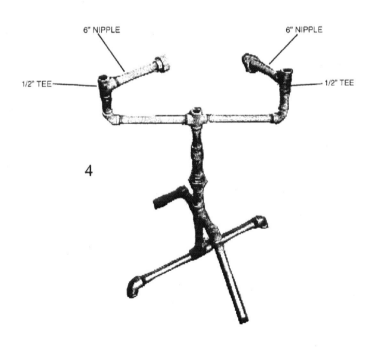

6" NIPPLE   6" NIPPLE

1/2" TEE   1/2" TEE

4

CONNECT SIDE SUPPORT FOR *SSMJ*

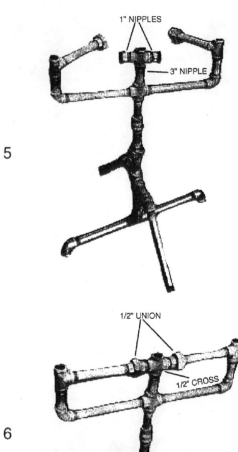

ADJUSTABLE STRIKE ZONE OF *SSMJ*

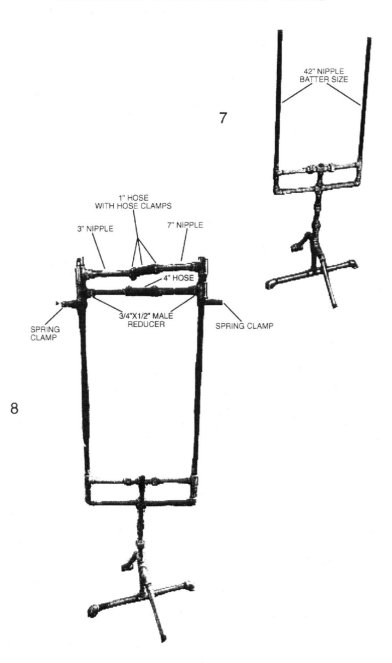

7

42" NIPPLE
BATTER SIZE

1" HOSE
WITH HOSE CLAMPS

3" NIPPLE   7" NIPPLE

4" HOSE

3/4"X1/2" MALE
REDUCER

SPRING
CLAMP

SPRING CLAMP

8

SSMJ WITH SEPARATOR FOR THROWING
* NOTE: ADVANCED THROWING ONLY

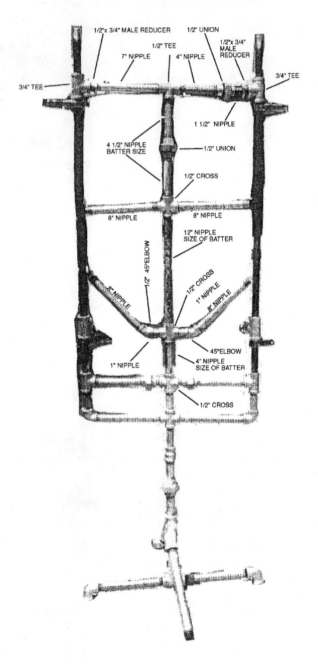

BASE FOR DIFFERENT *SSMJ* OR *SSMJC* ("*C*" FOR CATCHER)

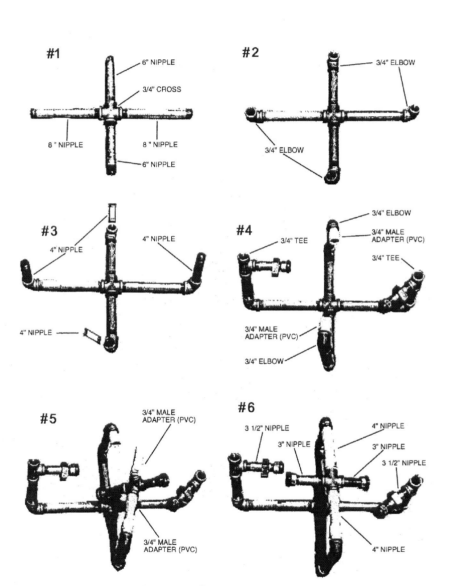

#1
- 6" NIPPLE
- 3/4" CROSS
- 8 " NIPPLE
- 8 " NIPPLE
- 6" NIPPLE

#2
- 3/4" ELBOW
- 3/4" ELBOW

#3
- 4" NIPPLE
- 4" NIPPLE
- 4" NIPPLE

#4
- 3/4" ELBOW
- 3/4" MALE ADAPTER (PVC)
- 3/4" TEE
- 3/4" TEE
- 3/4" MALE ADAPTER (PVC)
- 3/4" ELBOW

#5
- 3/4" MALE ADAPTER (PVC)
- 3/4" MALE ADAPTER (PVC)

#6
- 3 1/2" NIPPLE
- 3" NIPPLE
- 4" NIPPLE
- 3" NIPPLE
- 3 1/2" NIPPLE
- 4" NIPPLE

Base and Sides for *SSMJC*
(Resembling *SSMJ*)

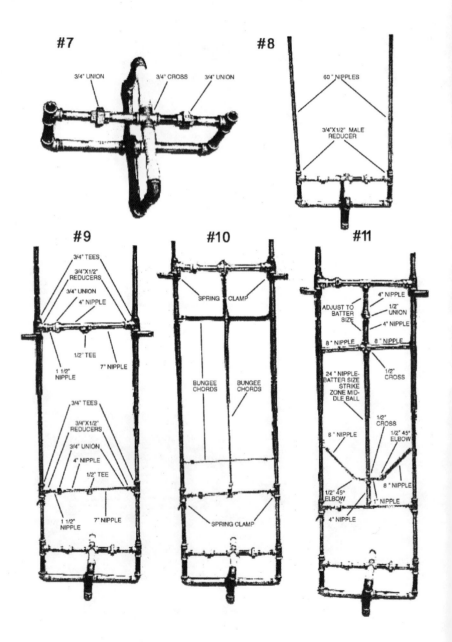

#7

3/4" UNION   3/4" CROSS   3/4" UNION

#8

60 " NIPPLES

3/4"X1/2" MALE REDUCER

#9

3/4" TEES
3/4"X1/2" REDUCERS
3/4" UNION
4" NIPPLE

1/2" TEE

1 1/2" NIPPLE   7" NIPPLE

3/4" TEES
3/4"X1/2" REDUCERS
3/4" UNION
4" NIPPLE
1/2" TEE

1 1/2" NIPPLE   7" NIPPLE

#10

SPRING CLAMP

BUNGEE CHORDS   BUNGEE CHORDS

SPRING CLAMP

#11

4" NIPPLE
ADJUST TO BATTER SIZE
1/2" UNION
4" NIPPLE
8 " NIPPLE   8 " NIPPLE
1/2" CROSS

24 " NIPPLE- BATTER SIZE STRIKE ZONE MIDDLE BALL

1/2" CROSS
8 " NIPPLE   1/2" 45° ELBOW
8 " NIPPLE
1/2" 45° ELBOW   1" NIPPLE
4" NIPPLE

*PRACTICE THROWING AND HITTING AT THE SAME
TIME OR TWO CHALLENGE MATCHES AT THE SAME
TIME MASTER HITTER OR MASTER THROWER*

SSM2 and *SSMJ* Connect as One Device

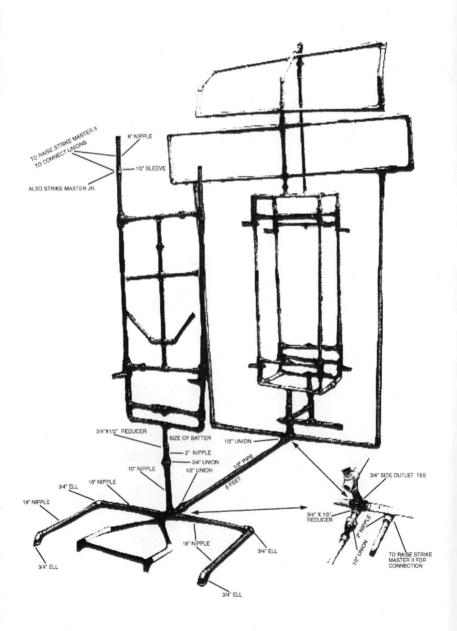

TO RAISE STRIKE MASTER II
TO CONNECT UNIONS

ALSO STRIKE MASTER JR.

6" NIPPLE

1/2" SLEEVE

3/4"X1/2" REDUCER

SIZE OF BATTER

1/2" UNION

2" NIPPLE

3/4" UNION

1/2" UNION

10" NIPPLE

1/2" PIPE

5 FEET

3/4" SIDE OUTLET TEE

18" NIPPLE

3/4" ELL

18" NIPPLE

3/4" X 1/2" REDUCER

2" NIPPLE

1/2" UNION

TO RAISE STRIKE MASTER II FOR CONNECTION

3/4" ELL

18" NIPPLE

3/4" ELL

3/4" ELL

SLIDE MASTER

913. What is the Slide Master?

It is a device to help the player practice base sliding without getting hurt. The Slide Master will help the player practice alone so he/she can perfect the way to base slide properly.

914. What is the purpose of the swinging ball?

The swinging ball takes the place of the base player. With this device, it lets the base runner understand and practice on how to get past the base player without being tagged by the ball. It will simulate the situation of being tagged by the base player with the ball, as if in a baseball game.

915. Is this the best way to practice base sliding?

The best way is to have five players: a pitcher, catcher, second base player, first base player and a base runner. But when can the base runner get that many players who want to practice just on base sliding? That is the purpose of the inventions. The player can practice alone and the player will have no excuse for not being the best base runner on the team.

916. Explain the pictures on the following pages.

When you practice with the Slide Master, you start swinging the ball. The objective is not to let the ball touch the base runner when he/she slides, otherwise the base runner is out. It is the same as if the base player tagged the base runner with the ball when sliding into the base.

917. *How do you swing the ball?*

> You adjust the ball to its lowest setting without touching the ground. Place the base behind the ball and swing the ball. Have a friend swing the ball and you can practice base sliding or you can do it by yourself.

918. *Can I swing the two balls by myself?*

> You can, but it will be a little difficult, for while the ball is swinging the base runner will have to run back the distance, then run and slide into the base. It can be done, but hurry. Add more metal washers to the ball will give you a little more time.

919. *Is base sliding that important in baseball?*

> Yes. Base sliding is just as important as hitting, throwing, fielding or any other activity. So, go practice to be the best base runner on the team. You can also have a friend play with you so he/she can swing the ball while you slide.

920. *Is it harder to slide past two swing balls than one swinging ball?*

> Yes. The two swinging balls make it more difficult to slide past. Remember, to read the chapter on Base Running before you practice with the Slide Master.

921. *Will it be harder to slide past a softball swinging than a hard ball?*

> Yes. The larger the ball the more difficult it is to slide past.

922. *How wide is the running path of a base runner?*

> The specific baseball summary rule regarding this states, "When the base runner is running in excess of three feet off a straight line to the middle of the bases to dodge from being tagged, except when his/her movements is to evade hindrance with a fielder who is fielding a batted ball, the base runner will be out." The Slide Master is the running path for the base runner.

923. *What are the steps on practicing base sliding?*

> Read the chapter on base running again, then start out using the Slide Master. Read the words near each picture and practice the way the most accommodates your style of base sliding.

924. Is the Slide Master dangerous?

> No. If you go practice where there is grass or dirt, such as a park, baseball field or even your back yard (ask your parents first). Again, use the methods in base sliding that are taught and you will not get hurt.

925. How do you assemble the Slide Master?

> First, buy all the materials. Second, assemble the Ball Swinger, cutting the plastic nipples to size, each of the plastic nipples are 6 inches long. Third, drill a hole in each of the baseballs of about 1/4-inch or larger for the nylon string to go through, with a metal washer or washers on the end so the knot in the nylon string will not slip through. Use as many metal washers as you like for the weight of the ball to swing. Fourth, thread the string as shown in the drawing. Fifth, at the 1/2-inch cross of the Ball Swinger connect the 12-inch nipples and 1/2-inch sleeves, or use one 3-foot long nipple, 1/2-inch pipe on each side of the cross. Sixth, connect the 3/4-inch by 1/2-inch reducers on each end of the 3-foot nipple. Seventh, use a 3/4-inch ell and connect to the reducers. Eight, for side support, connect the 12-inch nipples with the 3/4-inch sleeves, or use one 3/4-inch pipe, 4 feet long. Now, with the three-pipe base already constructed, spin the 3/4-inch side outlet tee on the 4-foot nipple and you are finished.

926. Why did you use 12-inch nipples and sleeves instead of one nipple size?

> It is easier to store and more portable, especially if you have a small car or bicycle to transport the Slide Master.

927. How can I make the ball swing for a longer time?

> Add more washers to the base of the swinging baseball and you can raise the Support Pole by adding more 12-inch pipe. In doing this, the baseballs will swing longer and more straighter like a pendulum of a clock.

PRACTICE WITH SLIDE MASTER OR CHALLENGE MATCH—MASTER BASE RUNNER

BASE RUNNER IS SAFE FOR NOT TOUCHING THE BALLS.   PRACTICE WITH THE TEAM OR FRIENDS

PRACTICE BASE SLIDING AND THROWING

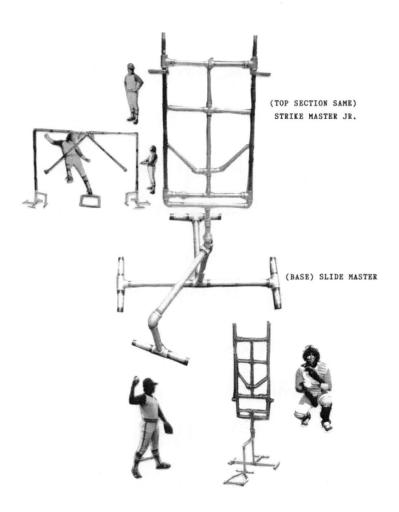

(TOP SECTION SAME)
STRIKE MASTER JR.

(BASE) SLIDE MASTER

BASE FOR SLIDE MASTER AND SSMJ

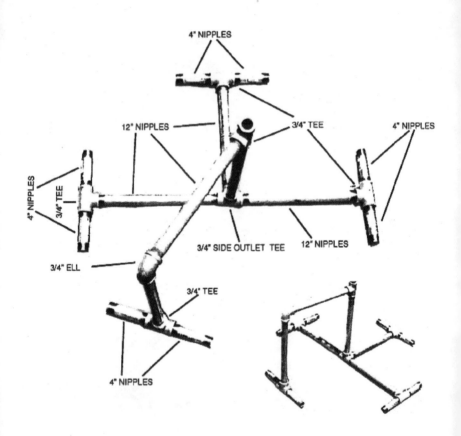

BASE FOR SLIDE MASTER AND SSMJ

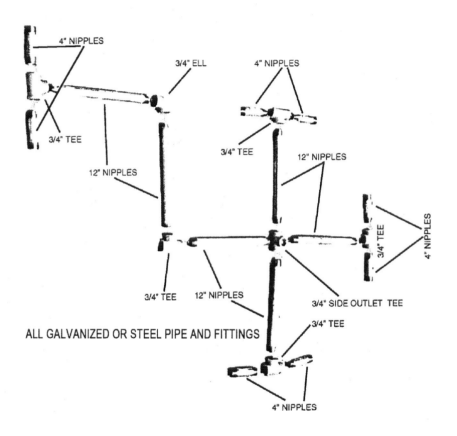

4" NIPPLES

3/4" ELL

4" NIPPLES

3/4" TEE

3/4" TEE

12" NIPPLES

12" NIPPLES

12" NIPPLES

3/4" TEE

4" NIPPLES

3/4" TEE

12" NIPPLES

3/4" SIDE OUTLET TEE

ALL GALVANIZED OR STEEL PIPE AND FITTINGS

3/4" TEE

4" NIPPLES

BASE FOR SLIDE MASTER AND SSMJ
TOP PORTION OF SLIDE MASTER

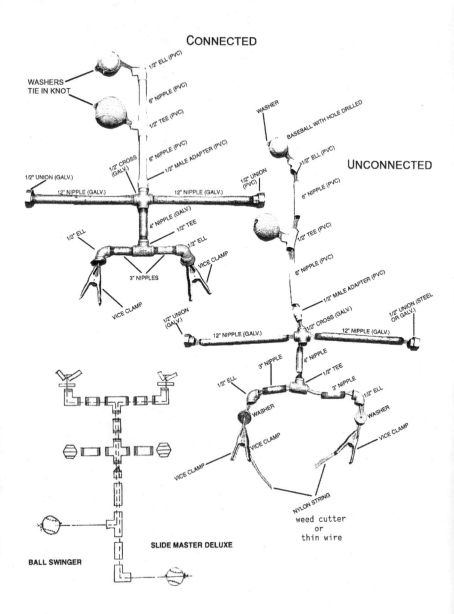

CONNECTED

WASHERS
TIE IN KNOT

1/2" ELL (PVC)

6" NIPPLE (PVC)

1/2" TEE (PVC)

6" NIPPLE (PVC)

1/2" MALE ADAPTER (PVC)

1/2" CROSS (GALV.)

1/2" UNION (GALV.)

12" NIPPLE (GALV.)   12" NIPPLE (GALV.)

4" NIPPLE (GALV.)

1/2" ELL

1/2" TEE

1/2" ELL

VICE CLAMP

3" NIPPLES

VICE CLAMP

UNCONNECTED

WASHER

BASEBALL WITH HOLE DRILLED

1/2" ELL (PVC)

1/2" UNION (PVC)

6" NIPPLE (PVC)

1/2" TEE (PVC)

6" NIPPLE (PVC)

1/2" MALE ADAPTER (PVC)

1/2" UNION (GALV.)

12" NIPPLE (GALV.)

1/2" CROSS (GALV.)

12" NIPPLE (GALV.)

1/2" UNION (STEEL OR GALV.)

3" NIPPLE

4" NIPPLE

1/2" ELL

1/2" TEE

3" NIPPLE

1/2" ELL

WASHER

WASHER

VICE CLAMP

VICE CLAMP

VICE CLAMP

NYLON STRING

weed cutter
or
thin wire

SLIDE MASTER DELUXE

BALL SWINGER

SIDE SUPPORTS FOR SLIDE MASTER
CONNECTED AND UNCONNECTED

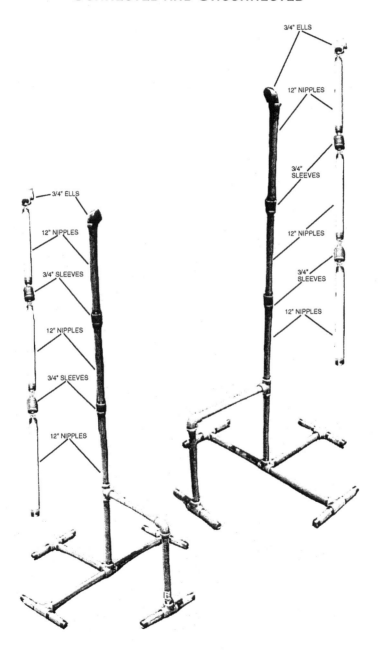

SLIDE MASTER—TOP SUPPORTS FOR BALL SWINGER
CONNECTED AND UNCONNECTED

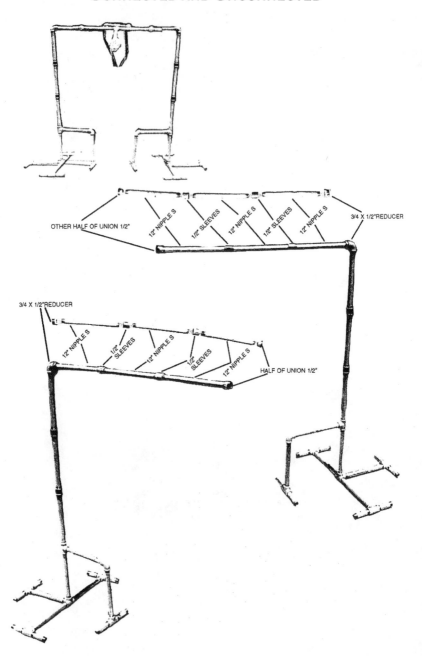

EASY PITCH BAT MASTER 1

928 What is the Easy Pitch Bat Master 1?

It is a baseball device used in Easy Pitch or Slow Pitch Baseball. The plate is identical in size to that used in Fast Pitch Baseball, but the ball is thrown high into the air over the batter's head in an arc. It will land on the plate for a strike. The Easy Pitch Bat Master 1 is used like the Tee Master and Bat Master. It will suspend the ball where it should be hit by the batter.

929. Why is the batter standing so far in back of the plate like in the picture?

This is the proper position to take for full plate coverage with the Bat Master 1 when going to bat. It is also the proper position to take on any Slow Pitch Baseball and the ball goes over the batter's head for a strike. On Slow Pitch, the batter will have to stand about 16 inches in back of the plate to have proper full plate coverage. As explained above in Fast Pitch, the batter cannot let the baseball get behind the swing, for he/she will have a late hit or will miss the ball completely. The secret of Slow Pitch is to let the ball drop in front of the batter. Then the batter will swing his/her bat at the ball. The objective of this is to get the "Hit Area" of the bat on the ball for a home run.

930. What are the rules in Slow Pitch Baseball?

They vary in numerous aspects, but many of the main rules are the same as in regular Fast Pitch Baseball.

931. *What are some of the dissimilar rules in Slow Pitch compared to Fast Pitch?*

> First, separate plate sizes for a strike. Second, various number of players, some have 2 players on each team or as many as 10 players on each team. Third, assorted sizes of baseballs. Fourth, multiple strike zones. Fifth, runners cannot steal a base or slide into a base, except home plate. Sixth, there are no balls, only strikes, so the batter cannot get a walk to base. Seventh, the ball is sometimes pitched a certain height in the air over the batter's head. Now, the player can get an idea of Slow Pitch Baseball. The players can basically have their own set of rules and there is not much chance of getting hurt with the ball, as in Fast Pitch. Whatever the rules are, Fast Pitch or Slow Pitch, the hitting and the throwing of the ball is essentially the same. Remember, that in hitting the ball in Easy Pitch, the batter must stand back farther, letting the ball drop in front of him/her.

932. *What is the only thing you want the batter to notice in the picture?*

> Look only at where the batter places the end of his bat for the proper plate coverage. The first 2 inches of the bat are extended to the other side of the Bat Master 1. This will line the batter up with the plate, simil ar to Question #65, except the batter is standing back 16 inches from the plate in the picture.

933. *What is the difference between Full Plate Coverage?*

> Using Home Plate, the batter cannot have full plate coverage without moving the batter's stance and stride while the ball is in flight. The batter will have such a larger stride that he/she will be forced to hit the ball incorrectly.

934. *With the Easy Pitch Bat Mater 1, will the batter have full plate coverage if he/she stands approximately 16 inches behind the plate as shown in the picture?*

> Yes. Once the batter takes the plate coverage and is ready at the plate, the batter will only have to stride and swing the bat. Remember, this distance is in back of the home plate. The batter must stand that far back, for the batter cannot let the ball drop in back of him/her. The ball must

land in front of the batter. There should be no movement of the body when the ball is in the air, except when the batter is ready to hit the ball.

935. *Then what is the advantage of having the ball land in front of the plate?*

First, the batter will have full plate coverage without moving forward and backward on each pitch. Second, the batter will not have a hitch or body movement while the ball is in flight for a late swing. Third, the batter will hit the ball correctly without any fault in his/her swing. Fourth, the batter will be able to play Fast Pitch without any changes in his/her hitting style.

936. *If the batter uses the old way of playing Easy Pitch Baseball, will it be difficult for the batter to hit the ball correctly or with the "Hit Area" of the bat?*

Yes. The batter will not hit the ball correctly. The batter will create a hitch or jerk motion in his/her stride and stance when adjusting to the ball as it comes down. Now, once the batter starts this type of movement action in the batter's stride and stance, plus any motion in other parts of his/her body, it will become a habit, and habits are hard to remove. The object of Slow Pitch, in our opinion, is to let the batter hit the ball. That is why we pitch the ball so slow. No matter how slow the ball is coming, if the batter has improper foot action or any body movements, the batter will not hit the ball hard, or will miss it completely. In addition, the batter will not be able to utilize any of the hitting inventions properly during batting practice.

937. *What if the batter steps out of the batter's box?*

That is illegal and the batter could be called out. Again, the rules may vary, but we recommend that there be no batter's box in Slow Pitch Baseball, except the distance the batter should stand away from home plate. The Bat Master 1 accounts for that distance.

938. *What are the advantages of using Easy Pitch Bat Master 1?*

First, the batter will hit the ball correctly for that home run. Second, if the batter decides to switch from Slow Pitch to Fast Pitch, then he/she can alternate without any different movements in the style of hitting. Third, the batter will be able to use the knowledge in this book to improve his/her hitting style to its finest level of hitting. Fourth, the batter will be able to stay completely still while the ball is in flight without having any twitches, knowing that he/she will have full plate coverage.

939. *What about the inside pitch?*

The batter must keep his rear arm up against the body to hit the inside ball. Remember, the more inside the pitch, the more the batter pins the rear arm to get the "Hit Area" of the bat on the ball.

940. *Could you explain the pictures on Full Plate Coverage.*

The batter swings the bat with the same type of swing as with the Tee Master and Bat Master. The pictures show how to use the Bat Master 1, but for the proper type of swing the batter must refer to the chapter on HITTING PROPERLY.

941. *Will the batter's batting style be the same for both Slow Pitch and Fast Pitch?*

Yes. In using the Bat Master 1, the batter will not be changing the style of hitting. Everything will be the same, except on Slow Pitch the batter will have to wait longer before his/she strides and swings the bat at the ball.

942. *I am a left-handed batter, can I use the Bat Master 1?*

Yes. Bat Master 1 can be used for either a left-handed or right-handed batter.

943. *In having the proper swing, what question should the batter refer to in the book?*

From the time the batter goes to bat, until he/she finishes the swing, refer to Question #193 for a summary.

944. *Why don't you have the 45° angle elbow in the drawing and the pictures?*

The 3/4-inch cross will be the stopping point for the batter's stance (NOTE DRAWING). The batter can use the 45° angle elbow if he/she chooses.

945. *How does a person assemble the Bat Master 1?*

It is assembled just like the Bat Master. Lay out the parts and then put it together for a lifetime of Easy Pitch Baseball practice enjoyment.

EASY / SLOW PITCH BAT MASTER

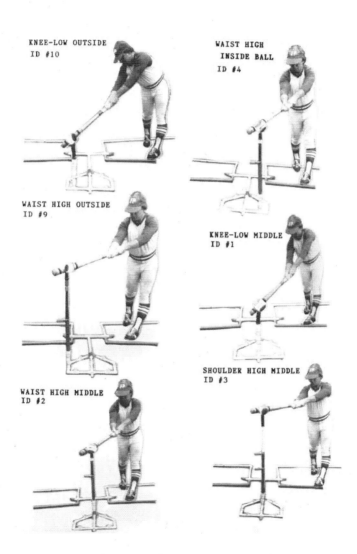

KNEE-LOW OUTSIDE
ID #10

WAIST HIGH
INSIDE BALL
ID #4

WAIST HIGH OUTSIDE
ID #9

KNEE-LOW MIDDLE
ID #1

SHOULDER HIGH MIDDLE
ID #3

WAIST HIGH MIDDLE
ID #2

EASY / SLOW PITCH BAT MASTER
ASSEMBLE

CONNECTED

UNCONNECTED

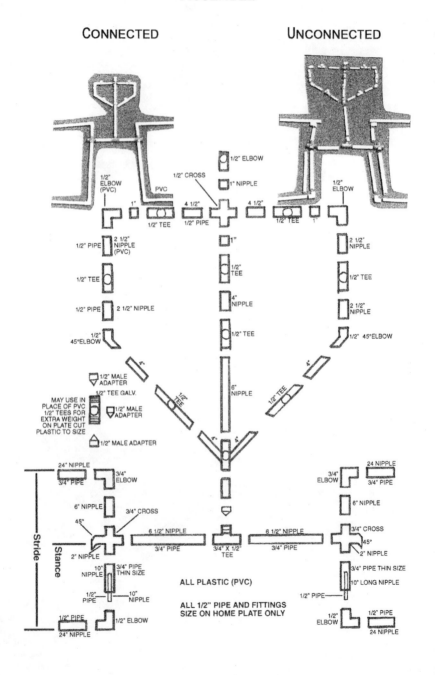

IN CONCLUSION

Now that you have read this baseball book, I hope you feel confident talking about baseball. Whether you are a coach, player or spectator, you can go head-to-head or nose-to-nose with the best of them and refute their disagreement with these baseball methods. Why? Because you can prove everything you say. You now have the ability to coach a team, teach your son or daughter, and demonstrate to your boyfriend, best buddy or anyone else who wants to learn the Art and Science of Baseball, hitting, throwing, infield, and outfield.

If you are playing a team that is not using these methods, you will beat them like a "hot knife cutting butter." Remember, when you debate baseball you want proof before you start talking about what is wrong with these methods. That means a device or invention that shows something.

Now, if you examine an automobile, show me a picture of the automobile so we can see which model is better. If you want to converse about an airplane, show me an airplane or a picture so we can decide which airplane is best. IF YOU ARE GOING TO DISCUSS ANYTHING—BOATS, TOOLS, CLOTHING, ANYTHING—SHOW ME A PICTURE OR DEVICE. AND AS OF THE WRITING OF THIS BOOK, THAT NOW INCLUDES BASEBALL!

If you ever pick up another baseball book, make sure it includes an invention so that that person can prove what he/she is saying. You are not interested in theories, guesses, assumptions, conjectures, speculations, or opinions. You want Statements of Fact, Truths, Certainties, and Realities, and to start that in motion you need a device or invention. I hope this is what I have done for American Baseball.

INDEX

All References are to Question Numbers

A

AVOID GETTING HIT
    Batter: 112-113, 134, 205, 207, 277
    Throwing the Ball: 352-353
    Pitcher: 439, 483
    Second Base: 539-542
    Catcher: 693-698-700
    Base Runner: 604, 764-765, 773-776
    Third Base: 604

B

BAD BALL HITTERS: 145, 158
BALK RULE: 744-745
BASEBALL BATS: 4-9, 82
    "Hit Area": 6, 65, 67, 69
BASE RUNNING: 449-500, 504-505, 736-783
    Practice: 760-764
    Head First Slide: 766
    Hood Slide: 767-772
    Scissors Slide: 768-769
    Hit the Dirt Slide: 770

INDEX of DEVICES